Farm Grown Leadership

Leadership Lessons from the Farm

E. L Luttrell
19929 E Victory Ln.
Sandy, OR 97055

www.cornerpostleadership.com   EdwardLLuttrell@gmail.com

Thanks

This book is the result of many people who have given me guidance and advice on leadership. To all who gave me encouragement and instruction over the years, I say thank you.

There are many who gave their suggestions and advice in the writing and development of this book. I appreciate their efforts in the proofing, editing, and many other tasks that go into the creation of a book. I give special credit and appreciation for the assistance of Gary Beller in helping me overcome some of my technical limitations. This book would not exist without his friendship and help.

Table of Contents

The Journey Begins

I am a storyteller, sometimes a good one and sometimes one who is striving to become better at it, but these few stories are shared in hopes that you will learn something that you will relate to your life. These stories will help you find and share your own stories of leadership.

Each of the following stories is focused on one word that I believe is important to a leader. While there are many more words that could have been included, just as I have many more stories; these are the ones that make up the core of my servant leadership style.

Growing up on a farm has impacted my life in so many ways. I spent my youth participating in 4-H (a youth program offered to children 9 to 18 through the USDA's Extension Service,) FFA (a youth program offered to high school students who take agriculture and related classes,) and the Grange (a family organization that includes members 14 years of age and older that serves primarily rural communities). These organizations challenged me to learn leadership skills. These lessons were learned because I was having a lot of fun. I have to admit that at the time, I often didn't understand the value of the lessons that were taught.

As a young adult, I found myself driven to become a leader. It was a goal or drive that I took seriously, even before I understood it. I desired to be treated as an adult and it drove me nuts when someone implied I was just a kid. I grew a mustache to look more mature and wore it for years, until I realized the years had taken care of that particular issue.

I studied leaders that I admired and soon found that I was sometimes imitating a trait or phrasing that seem comfortable or right. Learning from others became a habit. Sometimes I learned how to do something and other times I learned what not to do as a leader.

The next chapter of my growth as a leader happened when I had the opportunity to lead the Oregon State Grange (approximately 220 community organizations) and then later to lead the National Grange (approximately 2,000 local community organizations in 40 states). My appreciation and love of history had shown me the achievements of past leaders and encouraged me to attempt to become a visionary leader who attempted to lead towards heights unseen by many members.

Only later, as an experienced leader did I begin to take time to reflect upon what I had learned and experienced. My appreciation of those lessons of my early life in rural Oregon grew and has resulted in this book.

I don't believe that the lessons that I discovered in my journey are unique, but that each of us encounter these lessons in different ways. It doesn't matter if we read about a lesson, observe someone else or if we learn through practical experience. The important task for each of us is to recognize and incorporate these lessons into our lives.

The future of the organizations that we belong to depend upon each of us as leaders. It doesn't matter if you are the ranking officer in the organization or if you are just a member with an idea. When you step forward, you become a leader, whether you are ready or not for that journey.

The point of the journey of leadership isn't the end or destination. I believe that the point of the journey is the touching of lives along the way. It is about the people, not recognition, fame, or a legacy. One of the lessons of the Grange that I try to live by is that if we build grand temples, they will crumble into dust. If we work on brass, time will corrode it. However, if we work upon immortal minds, they will brighten unto all of eternity. The lesson is that we must share what we have learned so that others may benefit from it.

When you become a leader, it becomes your responsibility to the organization to gain as much knowledge as possible. This will ensure that those who look to you for leadership are part of the team which will create the path that leads to the best possible future.

Some of the stories in this book will make you smile, or maybe even laugh. A few may touch your heart. Each will offer a lesson that you can use in your personal journey of leadership.

Enjoy reading these stories and I hope that you find ways to touch more lives in your journey of leadership and life.

Accommodation

My 4-H project and our family milk cow was a Jersey named Charlotte. Being a 4-H project and a milk cow, she was very used to being handled. You could walk up to her in the pasture and she would just ignore you, unless you scratched or rubbed her itch, which usually was at the base of her tail. Of course, a treat consisting of a handful of grain or an apple would make her your buddy, at least until it was gone.

Every morning and evening that little Jersey had to be milked. Most mornings, my Dad milked her before going to work. In retrospect, I wonder if he didn't have confidence that I wouldn't miss the school bus. However, in the evening, it was my task to do the milking.

The first step of milking was to get the milking bucket and other items down to the corral. Then you would call for Charlotte. When she didn't appear, you would head to the pasture where the herd was that day.

As soon as you entered the field, she would head for the corral, unless she was crankier than usual. Occasionally, she would stand at the far end of the pasture and wait until you walked up to her, then she would start for the corral.

It didn't seem to matter if it was the end of a hot day or a cold rainy evening. Unless the cows were in a pasture next to the corral, a normal day consisted of a walk to collect Charlotte for milking.

She would go straight to the stanchion and check to see if you had fed her yet. As a milk cow, she got a small ration of feed grain with every milking. I think she somehow knew that she was special as she was the only cow in the herd to get some grain every day.

Once you were ready, you poured a ration of grain into the manger and shut the stanchion and start milking her. You had to shut the stanchion because she would finish the grain before you would finish milking and you didn't want her to try to leave.

When you finished milking, you cleaned things up, let Charlotte out of the stanchion, and headed back to the house with a bucket of milk.

It seemed to me to be unnecessary to have to walk out to the pasture to get Charlotte to come to the corral. It was irritating at times, because you knew that she looked forward to that ration of grain. Yet we walked out to get her almost every day.

We accommodated the stubbornness of that Jersey because we had fresh milk, butter, and ice cream because of her. The extra walk was just the price we paid to have fresh milk. Charlotte wasn't mean, just for some reason known only to herself, she wanted you to come get her.

As a leader, you will encounter members who irritate or frustrate you. Take the time to look at what they add to the team effort. Then gently accommodate them. Build a team that includes the talents and abilities of all the members.

Take the time to think about what motivates the difficult team member. Discover their passion and why they are a member. You may discover ways to strengthen their team spirit when you have a better understanding of them.

When a member drives you momentarily crazy, remember that just because you don't understand why they do whatever they do, it doesn't mean that they are not contributing to the team's success. Give them the benefit of doubt and accommodate their uniqueness.

Remember that the difference between one of your team members and a Jersey cow is that you can reason with your member. You might just be able to convince them to do things differently, unlike a stubborn Jersey cow.

Attitude

I learned my first real lesson in the power of attitude by watching my 4-H project. That project was a Jersey heifer (girl) calf that I named Charlotte.

My parents had a cow-calf operation made up of Charolais cross beef cattle. For the non-farmer, a cow-calf operation is where you have cows and they have calves which are produced for market. On our little farm, the calves were either added to the herd as future producing cows or marketed as quality beef to our customers. A Charolais is a white large beef breed and we had a number of cows that weighed approximately 1,600 pounds. We averaged about 10 to 12 producing cows and because they were crossed from dairy stock, we would have an additional 6 to 8 Holstein calves as second babies to the cows that produced too much milk for just one calf.

My dad brought the little Jersey home and if I remember correctly he paid $9 for the calf. I was nine years old and paid Dad $9 for the cute little calf. I decided to name her Charlotte as I had recently read the book "Charlotte's Web".

Charlotte was a bottle-baby as she had no mother in the herd. Due to that fact, we kept her in a small calf shed in the apple orchard and morning and night took her a bottle filled with milk replacer.

The weeks passed, and Charlotte became more pet than cow. Being my first calf, and a bottle-baby she looked to me and my parents as part of her personal herd. She grew quickly and became a teenage calf, eating a lot of hay and grass, but still looking forward to her bottles of milk.

The day finally came when it was time to introduce Charlotte to the herd. This marked the end of her life as a pet and begin her life as a member of the herd. By this time Charlotte may have weighed 300 or 400 pounds.

On the big day, with my Mom, I led Charlotte up to the herd where they waited to be let into a new pasture and then took her halter off.

We waited to see what would happen next. I expected several of the cows to investigate her by smelling her over and likely to show her that they were boss.

What happened was that Charlotte put her head down and charged one of the biggest cows in the herd. The old cow put her head down and met the charge of the tiny Jersey. I still remember that impact, the old cows' neck bowed as she absorbed the impact without moving a single foot. She then simply straightened her neck and flipped over that little Jersey.

That was my first inkling that Charlotte had a real attitude.

Over the next few months, Charlotte became part of the herd and enjoyed the lush grass and the supplemental bottle. As winter approached the herd was kept around the barn and fed hay that had been harvested during the summer. The reason for this was that the cows would tear up the wet pasture land if allowed in the pasture during winter.

While checking the herd, we noticed that Charlotte wasn't getting much to eat. We'd see her enter the feeding area and observed that she never failed to butt one of the cows or yearlings on her way into eat. Since all were much larger than her, they return the favor and run her away from the hay manger. Watching for a few days, it became apparent that Charlotte was not going to stop her behavior. She wasn't happy being at the bottom of the herd's pecking order.

It soon became a habit to take her a small bucket of grain to supplement the few bites of hay that she grabbed before being reminded of her lowly status.

The next spring, with the return to the pasture, life returned to normal. Time flew by and Charlotte was bred and she eventually had a little bull calf we named Wilbur. As a full-grown cow, she likely didn't weigh over 800 pounds soaking wet.

Despite being the smallest cow on the place, we noticed that she kept moving up in the herd hierarchy. Once we started watching her, it became clear that she had a strategy. Every spring as the new calves were born, she would often butt them and let each calf understand that she was not to be messed with.

As the months passed and the calves would grow larger than her, she would just shake her head at them and they left that aggressive Jersey alone and followed her lead. It is likely that they were just a bit afraid of the nasty-tempered old Jersey cow and had more than a few memories of what she'd do if they crossed her. Even as they passed her in size, they didn't want to take the chance that she'd remind them of who was boss.

Charlotte produced five calves and became the number 3 cow in the herd. Judging her by size, she should have been the bottom cow in the herd. However, because she did not accept her position based upon her size, her attitude became the measuring stick.

Attitude did not take her to the number one position, simply because Octavia, the herd leader, wasn't going to give up her position that she had won by size and strength. But she and Charlotte had a truce, Charlotte didn't challenge her and Octavia and her daughter didn't have to prove their position.

The lesson is simple. Attitude is as important to leaders as it is to cows. No matter where you start in life, your attitude will either carry you toward your dreams or prevent you from reaching them.

All your skills and abilities can only take you so far. Charlotte's attitude made up for much of her lack of size and muscle. Those cows who grew up bossed by Charlotte allowed her attitude to overwhelm their own desires of dominance in the herd. They surrendered to her because she was the boss.

Yet even Charlotte realized there was a limit to her rise, and rather than struggling pointlessly, she was satisfied to reach the top tier, but not the top position. This shows that you need to temper your own attitudes to reflect limits that you do not have control.

In your journey as a leader, remember that attitude is a tool that you control. You create your own attitude and then use it as a tool along with your skills and abilities. If you have a poor attitude, change it. If you have a great attitude, temper it with self-control.

If a little Jersey cow can use attitude to gain her goals, you can use attitude to achieve your dreams.

Challenge

When I entered high school, I chose to take vocational agriculture as one of my elective classes and quickly became a member of the Future Farmers of America association. Our chapter had only freshmen and sophomores in it as the school district had both a mid-high school and a senior-high school for the juniors and seniors.

The first contest was the creed speaking contest for freshmen. I remember the mixture of fear and anticipation of that contest. I didn't place first or second, which would have qualified me for the District competition. I don't think I was third or even fourth. However, I got the FFA creed out without forgetting it, which was a relief.

From that point on, I entered every contest that I was eligible to enter. It became a personal challenge to learn and prove myself through the many contests that were available.

I found that I was much better in cutting metal in half with a torch than welding it back together in the shop skills contest. In woodworking, once again, I was proficient in sawing boards in half, but lacked finesse in reassembling them into something new.

The joy of public speaking and of debate in the parliamentary procedure contest became very real for me. While it took years to refine those skills, those early contests gave me a passion for communicating and debating with others and eventually lead to teaching others.

My projects included my Shorthorn cattle, as I decided beef cattle were far less demanding than dairy cows. I received the beef proficiency award several times. Yet the real reward for me was showing at the county and state fairs.

The peak of my competition was when I bought an old registered Shorthorn cow. She produced the first calf that I registered as a purebred Shorthorn. During high school, I also matured as a showman and did well at the county fair.

My parents let me grow a few acres of barley one year as part of my project. I was a proud FFA member when my quart jar of barley placed at the state fair.

One year, my chapter advisor entered me in the state co-op contest during the state convention. This was just a test of knowledge on cooperatives, and there were a lot of fellow students in that room. The result was that I placed tenth. I always wondered how well I could have done with some extra studying. Yet that contest inspired me to learn a great deal more about co-ops, their history and workings.

There was one contest that I found that I had no aptitude for. I entered the plant identification contest and found a room full of leaves, seeds, and stems of plants. A few I knew, alfalfa, barley and such. However, I quickly realized that knowing a plant was a cereal grain, did not mean you knew which variety it was. I may not have been last in the contest, but I gave it a real run.

I remember the contest where my friend and I used a transit to determine elevation. We were cocky, because we knew that we were good and expected to place high. Yet at the end we were at the bottom. It was at that point that we realized we had used a rod marked in tenths rather than fractions. Likely we were dead on, but our measurements were wrong due to using the wrong rod. I learned the important lesson of double checking things after that day.

My senior year, I had the pleasure of being on the state winning soil judging team. Now some people might not see the challenge in walking into a pit and rubbing soil between your fingers, and even tasting a bit of it, but it was an opportunity to learn something new at the time and the knowledge has been helpful when preparing the soil for planting gardens and landscape plants.

Livestock judging taught me to evaluate animals based upon their intended use. Meat, milking capability, or wool were all measurable factors and were a part of judging the animals.

There were a lot of contests that I entered. Each taught me something new and expanded my knowledge. All of them were a challenge. For some, the challenge was to sit down and take a test on what you had learned. In others, the challenge was to study, evaluate, and write down your reasons for your placings. The ones that I enjoyed the most, required you to prove your knowledge and ability by putting a skill into practice.

Every leader must seek challenges. The FFA gave me many positive challenges and aided in my developing into the leader I am today. I have learned that it is not contests that give you the greatest challenges, it is life.

Marriage, jobs, volunteer organizations, they all provide a multitude of challenges that you must overcome; each must learn and refine new skills in order to achieve success. Often it is the challenges where you do not achieve success that offer you the greatest lessons. It is the act of trying to meet a challenge and learning from the experience that adds the greatest value to your abilities.

Accept the challenges of life as opportunities to learn and grow. You will become a better leader due to the challenges you accept.

Civility

On the farm the different animals treat each other per the basic rules of their species. Most have some social structure where the biggest or strongest dominate the group.

Chickens flock together and as a group will kill a weak, sick, or injured chicken. They don't defend each other from predators either. Cattle include all in the herd. Size, strength, and occasionally a bit of attitude will determine their ranking within the herd. The herd protects the weak or young up to a point. Dogs form packs and the alpha or lead dog is normally the biggest and most aggressive.

People are different than animals. We can be cruel to each other or show compassion and caring to others. The same person can be cold and unfeeling one day in one situation and filled with empathy in the next day in a different circumstance.

Leaders need to understand the level of civility that is expected in their organization and their role in enforcing that level.

The first step is to define civility. In my world, you can disagree strongly while being civil. Discussion and debate are ways we learn, grow, and even on occasion, change. Calling someone a degrading name or implying that they are less intelligent, that they don't fit in the group, or are somehow inferior to you are some of the ways that you lose civility. It can be as simple as ignoring them or as direct as a statement saying, "we don't care."

Over the years I seen great moments of civility and also moments where the lack was appalling.

I remember seeing a member who was passionate about an issue stand in a meeting and refer to a fellow member as, "the distinguished delegate from California which on this issue I must respectfully disagree with". This is how that individual showed respect and civility in a meeting during debate on a hot topic.

Once a presiding officer interrupted a speaker who was debating an issue and said, "I'm tired of hearing about this." The young speaker was furious as he believed he was just laying out the reasons for his position and the group could have lost him as a member for that single moment of lack of civility.

On one occasion, a leader organized a letter writing campaign to object to the actions that the organization was required to take. The result was a lot of letters that amounted to no more than hate mail. Members of that organization were told that the issue was one of personal bias rather than an issue of due process. That lack of civility and truth divided the organization and did great harm to it.

I have seen organizations that treated some leaders with discourtesy just because there were other leaders who chose to act outside the bounds of civility to achieve their goals. However, the results are never quite what is anticipated.

Once a local group invited a speaker to their meeting and another guest actually booed when the speaker was introduced. The members who were there were shocked and the group that had invited the speaker didn't know what to do. Fortunately, the speaker ignored the rudeness and proceeded with the presentation. The question that you should ask yourself, what would you do if that happened after you had introduced a guest?

No matter what the standards of civility are within your organization, or what standards your predecessor had, your standards of civility will guide the actions of most of the members of your organization. If you are a respected leader, members will follow your lead in how they treat others. It becomes your responsibility as a leader to ensure that you and those that you have influence over, treat all with the standard of civility that you desire the organization to have.

Organizations where the leadership does not set a good example or allows others to conduct themselves in a less than civil manner, always struggle. Over the years, I have seen many local organizations fail simply because of one member. That one member usually does not treat anyone who questions or disagrees with the "official opinion" with civility. What happens is that those members tend to drive off anyone who has a drive to accomplish something new or desire to learn and grow. Once the group is composed of well-trained followers, the slow decline continues and at some point, the group normally fails.

It is leadership's responsibility set carry out the standards of civility in their organization. The lack of civil behavior will have great negative impact on your group, just as an atmosphere of courtesy and respect will entice new members to participate in leadership roles.

Unlike the animals of the farm who follow their instinct, you have the choice of how you treat every member when you are a leader.

Commitment

On the farm, we had a Charolais/Guernsey cross cow named Goldie, she was probably about 1,400 pounds and produced milk like a dairy cow. That was the first problem. She was an excellent mother and her calves were always top notch. However, she gave so much milk that a newborn calf couldn't begin to drink enough, and she would often end up with Mastitis (an udder infection).

The second problem with Goldie was that she was a kicker. In fact, she remains the most determined, strong, and accurate kicker that I've ever seen in my years working with cattle. I'd say she was a NFL caliber kicker on a high school team.

To solve the first problem every year, we would buy a Holstein calf to serve as a second baby for Goldie. However, Goldie was committed to her own calf and would reject the other as an interloper who was taking precious milk from the mouth of her baby.

Over the years we tried every trick we had heard of or could think of. We tried covering the Holstein calf with placenta and the mucus of birth so that Goldie would think it was her own. It didn't work at all. Goldie probably though we were quite stupid about that one, after all she knew her baby.

So at least twice a day we would bring Goldie to the corral and put her in the headgate and force her to let the Holstein calf nurse. That was where the second problem of her kicking came into play.

We tried hobbles and Goldie turned into a pile driver. We tied one of her hind legs to the fence. Even when something worked once, it was hard to repeat. One time I remember we had successfully restrained the hind legs and that old cow tried to kick us with a front hoof. At the time, I had trouble believing her determination, but now I admire it.

It was strange in a way that Goldie was a fairly good-natured cow and was easy to work with, right up until you introduced that little black and white calf. Then she became a kicking fiend.

Over the years, her kicking did a lot of damage. One year, she caught my Dad in the knee on the first night of his vacation and put him on crutches for most of his vacation. I watched her break a rough cut 2 by 6 (a board that hasn't been planed or smoothed and is truly that measurement) in half. Each of us was kicked occasionally and the poor calves always got their milk, but they often earned it with a few blows.

Goldie was committed to her calf and she never gave in without a fight. It never got easier and after three weeks, the same routine and fight was put up by that cow as on the first day.

By the time we became sick and tired of dealing with her, her calf had grown enough to take care of the volume of milk she produced and we'd either have a bottle baby or sometimes one of the other cows would adopt the little black and white guy.

However, Goldie learned that we were just as committed to forcing her to feed a second calf as she was to feeding her own. She didn't understand that it was for her own good and she had more than enough milk for two calves.

We learned commitment with that daily battle with Goldie. We knew she was going to fight and yet that little Holstein calf had to have its meal or it would go hungry and Goldie would become sick. My parents taught us commitment to helping both the cow and the calf no matter what bruises we might get.

We learned to admire that old cow and never wavered in our commitment to ensuring her health.

When you accept a position of leadership, it is a commitment that you will need to honor. Hopefully you understand what you've got yourself into by accepting, but likely there will be a few surprises along the way.

That commitment may be tested by some of your members who do not understand why something must be done or not done. The most difficult thing many leaders face is explaining why doing the right thing, even when it isn't popular, is the best thing.

There may not be a cow kicking you, but you will possibly end up with an invisible battle scar and your commitment will add to your experience.

Consideration

I learned to be considerate to others from George. George was a female white cat that was a little older than I was. As a child, I don't remember a time without George. I'm also not sure how a pretty female cat came by the moniker of George, but George she was.

Consideration isn't a trait that I normally associate with cats. I sometimes wonder if cats remember that they were worshiped in ancient cultures and still think that they deserve that level of adoration. I know that the cats in my house today seem to think that my sole purpose in life is to run the can opener.

The reason that I am sharing this story is that George was considerate to babies and old people. My parents shared pictures and stories about putting me in a playpen and I'd slowly bounce it near the couch were George was stretched out. They tell me that I'd grab a tail or leg and drag that cat into the playpen with me. George never scratched me or complained. I'm amazed that a cat would let a toddler even get close enough to drag them into a playpen more than once.

I don't remember when life changed, but there came a day when George thought that I was old enough to know better and taught me that cats are dangerous hunters with weapons of their own. George always loved attention, but she didn't tolerate rough treatment. Except by babies. George seemed to know that babies and toddlers loved to maul her with love and affection and she never harmed one.

However, her consideration ended when you were old enough to know better and then you'd better treat her with respect.

Think about what it means to show consideration to someone who may never have taken on a certain task. How many people are considerate of the feelings of others who are shy or frightened by new experiences.

George had one other group that she showed consideration to. As my grandmother aged, she sometimes wasn't as gentle as she thought she was. One day I watched as she patted George on the head. I believe that she thought she was petting the cat, but George's head bobbed up and down with each pat as Grandma's hand bopped her on the head.

I knew that if I had tried to pat her like that, there would have been a row of bleeding lines on my hand. Yet she just laid there and purred as if Grandma was merely rubbing her fur. That is when I realized George allowed babies and old people to treat her in ways she would not accept from the rest of us.

Somehow, she realized that rough treatment could be a sign of love from certain people, and she accepted and returned it in her way. Yet to those that she judged to be to be old enough to know better, she demanded respect on her terms.

Think of your role as a leader. Do you give consideration and patience to those who are inexperienced? Do you cut people some slack when they make a beginner's mistake? Once a person gains some experience, do you then hold them accountable, both for recognition of achievement and to learn from their mistakes?

George wasn't human, she was a cat. One trait that I found humorous was that when a squirrel, chipmunk, or mouse got into the house, she figured it was our problem to deal with it. Anything outside was fair game and she proved herself a superior mouser over the years. But inside the house, it was our problem. Maybe she was just showing those pests that were brave enough, or stupid enough, to enter the house some level of consideration.

As a leader, you have an opportunity to provide consideration to those who have talents and skills. You can aid others with their people skills or share your experiences to teach them how to temper their words and actions. You have the choice to be considerate towards others, and unlike George, you shouldn't scratch those who should know better.

Courage

I remember during my childhood my little brother was, on occasion, a bit more reckless, or as I thought at the time, more courageous. Now when I say my little brother, that is only because I'm older. I don't remember a time when he wasn't almost the same height and a lot heavier. If it wasn't for the fact that I've always been quick on my feet, my mouth would have gotten me into serious trouble with him.

I remember watching from the ground as my brother climbed trees and would get the tree top waving by shifting his weight. As the tree top would sway back and forth, my brother would hang on to the top of that tree. I remember the mixture of envy that I had for his courage and fear that I'd have to explain how he fell out of the tree.

I remember when the creek that ran through our farm froze over. It was my brother that chose to walk across the ice. Listening to the creaking and cracking noises convinced me that there was no reason to risk falling through the ice into the cold water. Once again, I found myself wondering whether it was courage or something else that my brother had.

As we grew up, occasionally my brother would get into a fight with someone. He and I had been taught by our parents not to start fights. But if forced into it, we should be willing and ready to win. I never saw or heard of my brother losing a fight. He was big and tough. I knew he had courage.

I never got into a fight, mostly because I talked my way out of them; once or twice because I saw no way to win and walked away. I was tall, but thin as a rail. Being a farm kid, I knew I was tough as I'd been working hard and could keep up with the men. While there were those who might be stronger, I knew that I could lift or move anything that they could.

When my brother and I went out with bicycles, I could go faster, yet when going down a long hill, he would always reach the bottom first. There was always a point where fear of what could happen if I crashed would overpower my desire to go faster. As a boy, I would sometimes wonder if I had courage.

When I entered high school and joined FFA and the Grange, I suddenly had a smorgasbord of contests that I could enter. I entered almost every contest, participated in virtually every activity, and ran for a lot of offices.

At first, I lost more often than I won; or more accurately, once in a while I placed in the middle. As I gained experience, I began winning occasionally. I might lose a couple of elections, but then I'd win one and I'd dive into that responsibility.

One day, I realized that my brother had not followed my lead. Even though he was just as passionate about farming and cattle as I was, he had not followed me into the FFA or the Grange. It took me years to realize that he likely felt much the same way when he saw me standing in front of a group as I had while watching him swaying in a tree top. In other words, we thought the other was partially nuts to take such a chance.

Courage isn't doing something that is easy, it is facing something that is hard and still doing it. The first time I stood in front of a large group, I was terrified. Yet I did it again and found that it was easier the second time. I was a terrible speaker as a freshman in high school, yet by the time I was a senior I was starting to show a little promise.

Since those years as a teenager, I've entered a lot of contests and competed in many elections. Losing hasn't gotten any easier nor winning any sweeter. Yet the challenge of testing myself or allowing my name to be suggested for additional responsibility hasn't been impacted.

Courage isn't the success or failure of your effort. Courage is in engaging in the effort. One important component of leadership is having the courage to allow yourself to take the chance. Then once you have the opportunity, you need the courage to do the job. Many call themselves leaders, yet fail to have the courage to stand for their principles and just do the easy parts of the job.

I have discovered that having the courage to stand alone for what is right is part of the courage to stand in front of the group and be a leader. Courage isn't how others see it, but how you deal with the fear that stands in your way.

I'll never be courageous about heights. I can admit that and live with it. Yet over the years, I've found myself on tall ladders and working on roofs that I never felt comfortable on. In facing my fears, I've found courage.

Because of the courage that I found in facing fears, I learned that one can fail doing the job of leading others without physical harm. You will learn tremendous lessons when you have the courage to risk failure. By facing the very real fears of leading, one can become a courageous leader.

You may not have a younger brother to compete with, but life will give you many opportunities to learn how to identify and share your courage.

Curiosity

On the farm, just like everywhere else, there is always something new to learn or see. I remember one day I was sick and my mom had kept me out of school.

That day turned out to be unique in that a heifer was in labor. She had been in labor most of the night and that morning my mom came in to the house and called the vet. She checked in on me and as I was feeling a bit better, she directed me to get dressed and help her with the heifer.

We got a halter on the heifer and brought her up toward the house to be away from the herd. At that point I could see that the pregnant heifer was having serious contractions and yet there was no sign of delivery.

Soon Doc Kimball arrived and began his examination. His diagnosis was that the pelvis of the heifer was too small to allow the calf to be born. He was going to have to do a C-Section to save the calf and the heifer. I understood that a C-Section was a Caesarian birth and for a moment was glad to have woken up sick this morning.

The vet began by shaving the area of the heifer where he was going to perform the C-Section. Then he disinfected the area and then said, "now for something to relax her a bit." He gave her a shot and explained to me that a local anesthesia was more than adequate to keep the heifer from feeling pain.

He was explaining that with C-Sections on cattle were best done with the cow standing when suddenly, the heifers eyes rolled up and she collapsed. As we had positioned her on a slight slope, she ended up laying on the area which had been prepped for the operation. I remember someone saying that it seemed she was a little more tired than we had thought.

Doc Kimball shrugged and said that it appeared that we'd be doing this one laying down. Together we rolled the heifer down the slope so that shaved area was facing up. He then proceeded to redo his process of disinfecting the area.

Even though I'd seen many births, and helped with a good number of them, watching that C-Section was fascinating. It was done quickly and there was very little blood. In a few minutes, we were rubbing a new calf with a burlap bag and watching it get on its feet.

While we were getting the calf on its feet, the vet stitched up the new mother. We all felt great having seen both the cow and calf saved. That cow took a little while to shake off her lethargy, but having her baby to clean helped a lot.

The lesson that I learned was that curiosity was a good thing. Sometimes you are given the opportunity to explore something and other times you are thrown into a situation you're unfamiliar with. Asking questions is a good thing. Often what seems a stupid or silly question will open the door to real knowledge.

On the farm, we learned about the natural world because of our curiosity. Occasionally, a situation would arise that gave us the opportunity to see something new. A leader should be curious about the different aspects of leadership and always keep an open mind.

Every leader should develop a sense of curiosity. You should be always looking at ways to accomplish tasks easier. Listen when someone is describing how they solved an interesting problem. Ask other leaders how they dealt with a problem member.

Your curiosity is the beginning of a practical education, full of learning from others as well as knowledge from books and experience. No effective leader ever stops learning.

You may not get the chance to see a heifer have a C-Section, but you will have the opportunity to be curious and explore many other things.

Determination

Max was a Sheltie and a great little farm dog. A Sheltie is a dog that looks like a Collie, but is much smaller. Max's job on the farm was to be the watch dog and let his people know when something was out of place or when someone came onto the farm.

Max didn't herd the animals, but whenever we went to do chores or other farm work, he tagged along and kept us company. He was always there like every good farm dog. There were many times that his barking warned us that the cows were out, or something else was not normal.

The one thing Max didn't like was opossums. I'm not sure why he didn't like them, but in his mind, they did not belong on his farm. As a bit of background, opossums are not native to our farm's area and were considered by most to be varmints. They posed a danger to the chickens and competed for food from the native birds and animals.

Max's problem was in spite of his dislike of opossums, he wasn't big enough to do much to them. When he found one of the slow-moving opossums, he would start barking and usually it would play dead. He would bite it, being careful not to get too close to its teeth, but he didn't have enough size and strength to harm it. Opossum tactics were just to wait until whatever was bothering them got tired and then get up and continue with whatever journey they were on.

What set Max apart from many dogs that encountered an opossum, was that he was determined to eliminate the intruder. Once he started barking at an opossum, he was determined to finish his job.

There were many nights were Max would start barking and after a bit, either one of us kids or Dad would get up, get the flashlight, and go out to see what was troubling Max.

Occasionally, we would find Max barking and bouncing around an apparently dead opossum. We often poked the opossum with a stick as they would be playing dead. Once in a great while, we'd see Max circling an opossum that was baring its teeth and trying to intimidate him.

No matter whether the opossum was playing dead or being aggressive, Max wasn't going to let it go. They were on his farm and it was his job to protect it.

What Max was waiting for was for someone to go get the single shot 22 out of the gun cabinet. Max was determined to keep that opossum occupied until his family shot that varmint. After the shot, Max was content that the interloper was dead and he would head back to the house. Sometimes, he would grab it and shake it once, but then he was done with it.

Imagine a leader who is determined to carry out his or her duties. No matter what others say or what has been done by others, that leader works hard to ensure that their duties are performed to the best of their ability. If you can image that leader, you can be that leader.

You may not face huge challenges, but every leader encounters some difficult moments. The mark of a great leader is meeting that challenge, no matter how big or small. Like Max, you will find that challenge will sometimes be more than you can overcome by yourself. That is when the team that you've built accompanied with your determination will pay off.

Have the determination that little Max had to protect his farm. You will probably not have to fight off opossums, but you will need to develop the determination to do your job in the face of challenges.

Disappointment

Templeton was a Holstein steer I bought to have a market steer for the fair. (If you're wondering how a steer got the name of Templeton, my Jersey was Charlotte, her first calf was Wilber and as a kid I enjoyed reading.) One of the many books I had read and enjoyed was "Charlotte's Web".

A market steer is a neutered boy cow for those of you not from the farm, and is raised by 4-H, FFA or other youth program participants. The purpose of raising a market steer is two-fold. First the young member learns to care for the animal, keep records, learns about genetics and feeding programs, and learns economic reality. Second is the big livestock sale at the County Fair where the adults support the youth in these programs by purchasing the steer, lamb, or hog; often paying much more than market price to reward these young people for their hard work.

Heel flies, often called Warble flies, are a problem for cattle. They lay their eggs on the animal's legs above the hooves and when the eggs hatch, the tiny grubs crawl through the skin and over the next 4 to six months migrate to the cows back. There is medicine that kills these little grubs, but it cannot be applied too late or it can harm or kill the animal as the dead grubs can cause serious infections.

If not treated, the grubs create what looks like a giant zit on the animals back and you can see a tiny hole that it breathes through. You can pop the Warble out if you squeeze that zit. On our farm, we treated the herd so that that they would not suffer with these pests.

However, somehow Templeton missed his treatment, and the next spring, the giant zits of Warble larva erupted on his back. Everything seems normal until one day when Templeton started stumbling. It was as if his hind legs were not working correctly.

We called the vet, and his diagnosis was grim. From what he could tell, one of the Warbles was drilling into Templeton's spine. There was nothing we could do about it and that little grub doomed Templeton.

The loss of Templeton and the lost opportunity of having a market steer were emotionally hard for me. I remember thinking that it wasn't fair.

A few years later, I tried to raise another market steer. My parents had somehow ended up with a Scotch Highland steer. Being a bit of a rebel, I thought that the little steer would make a unique market steer. Now the Highland breed is native to Scotland and is a long-haired short-legged animal that is quite hardy.

He became a pet. I could lay in the straw with him, he was halter broke and well behaved. He was well-fed, and I knew that he might not be a big steer, but he'd stand out as different. My only worry was if he would make weight. Market steers have a minimum weight that they had to reach to be eligible for sale at the county fair.

One day, a few weeks before county fair, that pet steer just went nuts. He went after me and only the fact that he had his halter on gave me enough control to prevent my being injured.

I quickly realized I needed help and got my parents as I couldn't control that steer. That crazed steer dragged all of us and when we finally got him tied to something that he couldn't move, my parents had a talk with me. With him acting crazy, he wasn't going to the fair. We couldn't keep him on the farm either as he was now dangerous to us. The decision was made to take him to the slaughter house immediately.

We finally got him tied to the tractor and pulled him to where we loaded cattle into our truck. He was attacking the tractor and we all wondered what had changed a pet into a raging animal. When we got to the truck I went into the truck while my parents untied the steer from the tractor.

He saw me in the truck and charged into the truck to get me. I went up and over the stock racks before he got close enough to harm me. We shut the gate and that Highland steer went on his last ride.

We did some checking and found that some of the bloodlines of the Highland breed had an occasional animal that just went nuts. In remembering that day, it seemed that he had just lost his mind and gone insane.

I never tried to have another market steer for county fair as I was trying to build up my herd of Shorthorns after that. However, I do remember that feeling of disappointment that rose each year when the auction was starting. My eyes might mist up, but I knew that there was nothing that I could do about the situation.

Every person faces disappointments in their lives. Leaders often are faced with losing the vote on an issue, with having a team member create dissension or strife in the group, or even with losing an election and having to step down from the duties of a leadership position.

As a leader, you must learn how to be gracious in your disappointment. Accept the occasional defeat, be courteous when you lose, and especially don't let disappointment turn you bitter.

When you learn to be a class act, one who knows that disappointment is a part of learning and growing, you develop more empathy for others when you prevail and they do not. Learning to deal with disappointment will help you be a more gracious winner and a better leader.

Duty

Growing up on a farm that depended upon lush and healthy grass taught me responsibility and a sense of duty. Not only do you need to provide good growing conditions for the grass, but you work to prevent or minimize the growth of plants that crowd out the grass.

It is especially important to remove plants that are dangerous or poisonous to the cows. In the Willamette Valley, one of these plants is Tansy Ragwort. Tansy is a plant that damages grazing animals' livers and if they consume enough of it over time, the toxins are accumulative and they will die.

Cattle will seldom eat Tansy as a mature plant, but may easily eat it when it is young and mixed with the grass. Tansy spreads quickly and requires constant effort to keep under control. The problem on our farm was that the horse farm next door made little or no effort to keep Tansy under control. Each summer we'd watch as acres of Tansy would grow, bloom and spread their seeds in the wind, many of them drifting over the fence into our pastures.

My parents tried a variety of techniques to eradicate each seasons' new batch of Tansy. Spot spraying, the release of cinnabar moths (a moth whose larva would eat Tansy), and the tried and true method of digging each plant out of the ground.

As soon as we were big enough to begin to help, my Dad gave each of us a pocket knife. It wasn't a particularly good knife, it just had a good sized main blade. We were taught to dig up the Tansy and make sure that we got the roots. It was a rare day that you didn't stop and dig out a Tansy when walking around the farm.

My parents began by giving us each that pocket knife and a burlap feed sack. They explained the deal to us simply. They would pay us a penny for each Tansy we dug; provided that the roots were still on the plant.

I remember many an evening and uncounted Saturdays spent walking a pasture, digging up little Tansy plants. It seemed to take

31

forever to get a hundred plants in that bag, as little Tansy plants don't take up all that much room in a burlap feed sack. Unless you found a more mature plant, you knew the bag would have a lot of room, as the small plants pack down easily.

Our parents mostly took our word for how many we'd have in the bag. However, every now and then they'd dump the bag and glance through the pile to ensure that the entire plant was there, roots and all.

In reflection, I think it was mostly show for the purpose of teaching, but at the time I was sure that they were counting each plant to make sure that we were accurate in our count. Yet after every bag was dumped, they paid up; a penny for each Tansy.

One bonus is that if that cheap knife (I am fairly certain my Dad didn't pay much for them) broke, you got a new one. For our family of little capitalists, it was a great opportunity, the neighbor seeding our pasture, a free knife, and a burlap bag and a penny for each Tansy.

As a little kid, digging Tansy was the only chore or duty that I remember being paid for. Gathering eggs, feeding hay in the winter, fixing fence, or feeding the bottle babies were just chores that had to be done. I have no idea how much I earned over the years digging those Tansy, but it was a cash operation for us kids.

As we grew older and started acquiring cattle, such as my 4-H Jersey, digging Tansy became part of the rent that we paid for pasturing our cows. It also changed our attitude toward that neighbor. They were now endangering our own animals.

The lesson of responsibility and duty was begun by our parents when they explained why we needed to dig Tansy out of the pastures. The payment was simply an added incentive for young kids who were still sorting out doing the right thing.

The level of duty and responsibility changed when each of us got our first calf. The duty went from a "it's the right thing to do" and "this will get me a candy bar" to "this will help keep my cow healthy."

The lesson that you should take away is that everyone learns duty in stages. Providing people with incentives to do the right thing is smart and helps them learn. As they grow and learn, soon the incentives are not needed and they will assume the responsibility to their duties and meet the challenges that they face.

As a leader, you have an obligation to do the duties of the position you accept. You also are given the opportunity to teach your fellow members about doing their duty in the organization.

I must admit, those lessons of duty were deeply ingrained and to this day, it is very difficult to walk by a Tansy and not dig it up.

Educate

Every mammal needs be educated on how to survive and flourish. Cats are no different than any other animal on the farm.

A number of years ago, we bought a foreclosed house on one acre. The property had not been kept up for more than a year. While it was a great deal financially, it also required a lot of work to make it livable.

Once we got the house livable and moved in, I began mowing the lawn. The nearly one acre of lawn was no longer really a lawn. The grass was waist high and we referred to it as the prairie.

I had a powerful commercial quality push mower that I had bought used. I would fire up that mower and spend a few hours pushing it into the grass a few inches, backing it up to let the engine regain its speed and pushing it forward into the tall grass again until it started to lug down.

When we moved in, we brought two cats with us. Buddy, a long-haired black fixed male who was middle-aged. Buddy was death on four legs to mice and assorted rodents. The other cat was a grey kitten that came from a litter that had been found dumped in a box in a ditch. She and her mother and siblings had been found dying in a box by a sister-in-law and nursed back to health. As my daughter was staying with her aunt while attending college, it didn't surprise anyone when she brought a kitten home with her.

The little grey kitten dashed under the bed when she arrived and soon acquired the name Fuzz, due to her resembling a dust bunny as she hid under the bed. Slowly she got used to us and to Buddy.

As I mowed each day, more and more yard appeared. I found many broken toys and occasional boards and rocks. I did see that a multitude of mice, voles, and other assorted rodents which had set up living quarters in the protection of the tall, thick grass.

Buddy quickly realized that if he hung around near the noisy mower, he would have more opportunity to successfully hunt. I think it was because he really didn't have to hunt, it was more of a short wait for the next panic-stricken rodent to dash toward him. That was normally the last decision that rodent made.

First Fuzz checked out his kills. She'd play with them a little and she watched Buddy from a distance. She slowly edged toward the noisy mower until the day came when a terrified little vole almost ran into her. I saw her leap at it and she went around in a circle a couple of times, and then stopped as if wondering where the rodent had gone.

Over the next few weeks, Fuzz watched Buddy make kill after kill. Soon she was imitating him and having similar success in her hunting. One evening, I found Fuzz pulling baby moles out of a hole and knew that she had graduated into as effective a mouser as her teacher, Buddy.

Neither cat ever got near enough to the mower to make me concerned for their safety, but both got used to the noise. They both stayed close enough to deal with many of the little rodents whose life was disturbed by the process of converting wild prairie back into lawn.

An interesting thing is that once I completed mowing the tall grass down, neither cat ever came near the mower again.

Every leader needs to learn a wide variety of skills if they wish to be an effective leader. The first thing you must learn is that no one is a born leader. We all learn leadership skills from a combination of book learning, watching others, and trial and error. Just as cats learn their skills by watching and trying, a leader learns though a combination of learning techniques.

Take the time as a leader to ensure that you are always learning. Read books, blogs, and articles on leadership regularly. Observe other leaders and see what they do that works, or sometimes more importantly, what doesn't work. Then put your ideas into practice and evaluate what happens.

Just as Fuzz went from a clumsy kitten to a deadly hunter; you can progress from a new leader to a respected and successful leader when you have the desire and willingness to learn.

Embarrassment

Max was our Sheltie farm dog. The lesson he taught was that no matter what the embarrassment, you can still get the job done. It seemed like every summer Max would have two incidents where he became embarrassed about himself.

The first was when he suffered sunburn. Max looked just like a little Collie and had a nice wet black nose. However, his skin was pale and the hair on his muzzle was thin and light colored. Every summer it seemed that he would develop a sunburn at least once, right behind his nose.

The solution was iodine, which prevented any potential infection and added a bright purple layer of protection from further sunburn. Plus, it didn't need to be reapplied very often as it was a persistent purple.

After his "treatment" Max would be mortified that he suddenly had a purple nose. If someone pointed at his nose, he would even lay down and put both paws over his nose. Yet he'd forget his nose the moment that someone entered the driveway or if it was time to do chores.

It was only when there was nothing to do that he was embarrassed about his purple nose and even then, after a while he got used to it. I'm sure that he was relieved with his nose faded back to the color of his fur.

The lesson that Max shared was that being embarrassed is normal, but it shouldn't stop you from doing your job. If you are supposed to bark at any car that pulls onto the farm, it doesn't matter what color your nose is, you bark so that your family is aware of the car.

The second occasion when Max was embarrassed was when he got his summer haircut. Max would put up with whatever was needed, but when he heard those clippers, he'd get a resigned look about him.

We'd get out the trimmers we used on the show cattle, and shave off a large portion of Max's thick hair. We'd cut out matted patches of hair and trim him up so that the summer heat wouldn't be so hard on a busy farm dog.

When we'd finish giving Max his annual haircut, he would slink away from the pile of hair that we had just removed from him. Max always acted as if he was almost naked for a little while.

However, soon Max would realize that he could feel a breeze and then he would forget his embarrassment. Often something would demand his attention as the farm dog and his embarrassment would disappear. He would then enjoy running without the added weight and warmth of his winter coat.

This lesson was that often we're embarrassed by something that turns out to be beneficial. It is normal to feel embarrassed when we are outside our normal comfort zone. Yet embarrassment is usually just temporary and disappears the moment others join you or you become occupied in a task.

The challenge for every leader is to work through their moments of embarrassment and fulfill their duties. Embarrassment fades quickly as you get used to the situation and then you may discover that often you had no reason to be embarrassed in the first place. At that moment, you will have grown as a leader.

In addition, being a good sport will aid you in getting though many embarrassing moments as a leader. You hopefully will never experience Max's dreaded purple nose.

Focus

Trumpet was a Beagle mix unfixed male dog. He was my Grandmothers and Aunts dog and was getting along in dog years. He was content to stay near the house and take life easy. As background, I grew up across the road from my Grandmother and my Aunt who shared a house.

However, when a female dog was in heat (fertile, ovulating), Trumpet was focused on only one thing. He was convinced that he was just what she needed.

One morning I crossed the road to check in on Grandma and found my Aunt somewhat frustrated. Seeing me, she asked if I wanted to go with her to pick up Trumpet. I asked where he was, and she replied that he was up on Chehalem Mountain.

It was a least 4 miles by car and had to be nearly 2 miles in a straight line from Grandma's place to the farm where he was. We got in the car and headed up the Mountain to bring Trumpet home.

We got to the farm and were greeted warmly. We were led to the barn where Trumpet was penned up. He was a happy dog when he saw us. I loaded him into the car, although he wanted to visit the other dog that could be heard barking from the porch. I heard my Aunt thanking the nice couple for keeping Trumpet from harm.

Once in the car, Trumpet settled down and started to snooze. On the way home, my Aunt and I talked about the route that Trumpet might have taken. He had to cross at least one stream and likely two roads.

The going was mostly uphill and included both woods and fields. The dangers he might have encountered included coyotes in the fields and woods and cars on the roads. Since he was a fairly small dog, many of the farm dogs in the community would have been too much for him as well.

Trumpet had to get through fences, cross ditches, and work his way through brier patches. If he encountered an obstacle that he couldn't go through, he had to find a way around it. Any coyote or an eagle or even a large hawk might have taken a chance to make a meal out of him. Even without considering the dangers of a small dog trekking through the fields and woods, the challenges that his short legs faced were significant.

Once we got home, we let Trumpet out and put him in the garage for next couple of days. He was a tired old dog and slept well. Afterward he went about his business of watching over the house and grounds like every good farm dog does.

Up to his final day, when he scented a female dog in heat, he had to be kept in the garage or he would set out on his next adventure.

The lesson that Trumpet shared with us was his incredible focus on his single goal. As a male dog, he considered it essential that he overcome every obstacle to do his duty for the species. He was focused on his goal.

As leaders, we are not driven genetically like Trumpet to perform our duties. However, we can choose what we are going to focus on. We can focus on serving others, abiding by the rules, operating with specific ethics, or building a team.

Our focus can be on people, tasks, or both. Focusing on our duty or obligations is a part of what leaders should consider their priorities. Imagine if every leader was as focused on achieving their goals and objectives as Trumpet was in reaching one lonely female dog.

Fun (and Enjoyment)

Most animals on the farm take the opportunity to have fun when it is offered. The young especially, enjoy and celebrate life with fun.

Calves will race around the field, kicking up their heels, and having a great time having fun. If you watch a cow that finds a low branch, a sturdy post, or a person who is willing to scratch whatever is itching, you'll see true enjoyment.

Some dogs will play fetch for as long as you'll continue to through the ball or stick. Others will run around the house or barn just for the sheer joy of it. Young or old, dogs like to have fun.

A cat will take pleasure in playing with a mouse. That same cat will later crawl up in your lap and demand that you pet it while it kneads you with its front feet and sometimes its claws. I like to refer to that action as fluffing, not that I enjoy the pokes of their claws much.

Having fun on the farm isn't always about games. There are moments where the wonder of life is front and center. Watching a squirrel that doesn't know you're watching it. Seeing a doe lead her fawn down a path. Seeing a cat curl up with the dog on a cold night. Watching a new mother cow cleaning her calf.

Sometimes you make a mistake and others laugh at the situation. I know that I've offered others a great deal of humor with some of the mistakes I've made. I've opened bags and got a face full of dust as the bag ruptured rather than opening. I've reached for bottles and instead just knocked them over.

Here are four simple rules on fun for leaders.

1. If you're not having fun, your members don't have permission to have fun. This means you need to smile and set the example so that your members know that it is ok to have fun.

2. Be careful that no one is the butt of the joke. If you're going to pick on anyone, use yourself as the target. While some of our

members provide great sources for humor, remember that others may view those jokes as personal and that is never good for the team.

3. Only solemn or sacred moments should be fun free. The rest of the meeting, activities, and events should include fun as part of their agenda. Fun is a critical component in keeping members involved and energized.

4. Encourage people to laugh and share the humor of life. It makes the tough times bearable, the tedious activities less so, and good times better.

Leadership is about empowering others. Sharing fun and enjoying the company of others while doing something necessary or performing an important task. Fun is a task that every leader should pursue.

You may view a video of a farm animal having fun and laugh your socks off or you may find that people provide far better entertainment. You can tell jokes, riddles, or puns, share humorous photos and videos, or you can encourage others to do those things.

It does matter if you can add fun and enjoyment or if you allow these things; because that is what will help your members look forward to activities in your organization.

Become one of the successful leaders who include fun as part of their duties.

Hard Work

My mom wouldn't have a cow on the farm that wasn't halter-broke. That meant each calf was introduced to a halter and taught that the halter was necessary, and the calf had to accept the control that the halter represented. The halters we used were heavy leather, unlike the show halters we used on our 4-H and FFA cattle that we exhibited.

By halter breaking the calves, it taught them that the people on the farm wouldn't hurt them. It built trust as well as teaching the calf that they had to follow direction from the people. Getting calves used to the halter also gave us the added advantage of being able to touch and assist the calf in later years when they needed our help with health issues or found themselves in a situation where otherwise they might be harmed.

All our cattle were used to people working around them. The calves saw us change irrigation pipe every morning and evening, they saw us pet the 4-H and FFA show animals, and they saw us feed the herd or individual animals.

Halter breaking was normally done at the time we weaned the calves from their mothers. We had a corral and would run the calf into the head gate and put the unfamiliar halter on the calf. These calves were about 400 to 500 pounds. We would then turn them into the main portion of the corral.

The halter would have a heavy rope attached to give us some control. Now the key to controlling a calf or cow with a halter is to never let them head directly away from you. If you can control the head, you can keep them going in a circle until they realize they are not being hurt and eventually they choose to accept the halter and your control.

Being a tall skinny kid, I wrapped the rope halfway around me so that when the calf hit the end of the rope, the rope was under my rear. This meant that I was using my legs instead of my arms to turn the head of that calf.

That calf would try to dash away and it was my job to turn him or her. Those calves always fought the control of the halter for a while. On the rare occasion where they got their head turned away, you let go of the rope or were dragged by the powerful young animal.

Halter breaking was hard work. The young animal was much heavier than you, and they had four legs digging in the ground instead of just two. Knowing how to control the head was the key to having a chance at being successful. However, you knew that you might get stepped on, get a rope burn, or get hit with the stray flying dirt clod.

The task of halter breaking was always hard work. You stressed every muscle in your fight with the young heifer or steer. Some were more stubborn and tested your stamina before giving in to the inevitability of the halter.

The reward for this hard work was a sense of satisfaction in teaching that young animal that you could control it with the halter. The long-term success meant that if the animal was ever injured or sick that you had a way of getting it to where it could be helped. It also meant that it realized that people wouldn't hurt it. They knew that their people had the halter and had proved themselves to be in control. This could very well prevent an injury to someone in the future.

I cannot remember every having a young animal hurt during the process of halter breaking, but it was not unusual for the person to collect a few bumps and bruises in the process. I do remember, as a teenager, the pride in doing a man's job on the farm.

While I've never tried breaking a horse to ride, the process of halter breaking reminds me of the effort necessary to tame an animal much larger than a person.

As a leader, you will sometimes encounter a task that requires a lot of hard work. As the leader, you must set the example. Make sure no one gets hurt, and let your members test themselves with the goal that they will feel the satisfaction of completing a difficult task.

Finally, celebrate the completion of a task that requires hard work. When they complete such a task, it gives your members confidence and pride.

As a leader, sometimes our members make me long for a halter to guide them, but you can't halter break people. You must work hard to share the reason for the desired action and teach them gently. The friendships you make doing hard work with others make life truly a joy.

Honor

Honor isn't a trait that I've observed in animals. They operate on instinct and in reaction to the world they live in. Fight or flight, the mating drive, hunger, and other factors drive much of the behavior of the animals on the farm, in the wild, or in the house. They do have fun, show that they are curious, but an individual sense of honor is something that I've never seen.

People are different. We do have a sense of honor. My parents, grandparents, other relatives, and friends taught me that honor is something that you have control over. Telling the truth, having personal integrity, and doing the right thing in your dealings with others are part of being a good person with a sense of honor.

It has been said that honor is when you do the right thing, even when no one is watching.

Having honor doesn't mean that you don't make mistakes. What it means is that you do your best not to violate your core principles and when you do, you regret it and do your best to repair or fix what you've done wrong.

Many years ago, I had the opportunity to hire a person. Among the applicants was a man with the qualifications that the position required. He had been working with a church and seemed like a great guy. During the interview, he volunteered that he had served time for armed robbery. After volunteering what he had done, he asked if the interview was over. I told him no and proceeded to ask several more questions about the work he had been doing and why he wanted to work for our organization.

When I offered him the position, he was surprised and asked why I had chosen to hire him. I replied that he had paid his debt to society and from what I could see, he was an honorable man. He did a great job for us and I was sorry to see him leave later for a position with a church.

The lesson that should be taken from his story, is that no matter what the mistake, you can still choose to live your life with honor and dignity. Some may not forgive, but you can do the right thing and live the rest of your life with honor.

I have seen some leaders who think that their private lives have no bearing on their public duties or that they can smear their opponents without harm to their own reputations. Sometimes they are right, we see many politicians who do things that are not right, yet are re-elected.

But the difference in most of the non-profit world, and a sizable part of the business world, is that you can lose the trust of those you work with, or for, if you don't conduct yourself with honor. When you lose the trust, you lose far more than an election or position.

Leaders need to know what their own personal code of honor is. Honor is not situational or only around when convenient, honor is consistent and constant.

Your code of honor may come from your religious teachings. Things like the golden rule are foundational for many people. Your honor may have been taught to you by your family. It may have developed due to your experiences and from reflection on what makes life worth living.

The final point about honor is that your honor or ethics is the honor and ethics of the organization while you lead it. If you are truthful and demand that your officers and representatives are truthful, then the organization will be truthful. That is due to your members drawing their conclusions about what they should and shouldn't do from your actions.

As a leader, reflect on your honor and then live it in all aspects of your life. When you do err, which all humans do, reaffirm your honor by choosing the do the right thing to fix the mistake and avoid it in the future.

You are special, you have the ability and obligation to develop and live your own set of standards of honor.

Hope

As a senior in high school, one of my projects for Vocational Agriculture (the class which qualified you for FFA) was raising barley.

My parents let me use a field of about 5 acres to raise a crop of barley. I don't remember why I chose barley or what the rent for that field was. What I do know is that hope was one of the lessons that I learned from that field.

I began by plowing and disking the field. That was the same as preparing the soil for any crop that we raised, and I enjoyed the process of preparing the soil. The difference came when I paid for the seed. What you understand as needs and requirements for the seed when planted in the soil, suddenly become serious worries when you have a sizable investment in that seed.

I don't remember where we got the grain drill (the machine to plant the seeds) but once the barley was in the ground, the wait began. It takes a bit for the seeds to germinate and then for the green sprouts to burst from the soil.

I never had much patience, but it was agonizing to see nothing in that bare field. Hope was there and while logically I knew that the seed would germinate and grow, the anxiety of waiting to see the green plants emerge was strong.

Soon my hope was rewarded as the field was covered with green shoots bursting from the soil. Then the hope began that we would have spring rains, but not too much rain at one time.

The barley grew steadily. The rains came and went, and there was no extreme weather that would have damaged the growing plants. The young plants soon reached my ankles, then continued to grow to my knees. When the stalks were about waist high, my hope shifted to seeing the heads on each stalk fill with grain.

My hope was fulfilled as the top of each stalk filled with barley grains. Then once again my hope shifted. I hoped that the summer heat would ripen the grain and that we would not have a storm that would damage the tall plants. I realized that I could lose a sizable portion of the crop if a sudden wind storm flattened part or even all of the field.

Yet my hope remained strong. The summer passed and the barley ripened into a field of golden grain. I contracted with a neighbor with a combine to harvest the crop and I hoped that the field would be harvested before a rain came and possibly reduced the value of the crop.

Soon the combine arrived and began its slow laps around the field. Each circuit was smaller as the amount of waving grain steadily shrank. Some of the grain was bagged in burlap feed sacks and much of it was driven to town for sale to the co-op.

As the combine left the field, all that remained were windrows of barley straw. I greased up the baler and then baled that straw. The straw was then hauled to the barn and stacked near the hay, waiting for winter use.

As the final step of my project, I sorted through the grains of barley and filled a quart jar with the best of the grain. I hoped that the jar filled with barley would place high at the county and state fair.

Agriculture is filled with hope. At times, you hope for rain and at other times, sunshine. Not every hope is realized as life can and does have disappointments. Yet hope breathes life into goals and fills the mind with anticipation and optimism.

Every leader needs hope and to share that hope. When people have no hope, they give up, they put forth no effort. Yet when a group has hope, they often achieve great successes. Hope is a leaders' greatest tool in building a team.

Look for hope in every project or activity as a leader. Share the hope, what others may call a dream, with your fellow members and inspire them to work to achieve it. Even when the sky fills with clouds, have hope for the future.

You may not have a spring and summer of hope end up in a jar of barley being judged against other jars of grain, but as a leader, you will achieve more with hope.

Humor

As a nine-year-old boy, I bought a Jersey calf from my Dad for $9 as my first 4-H project. Because I had recently read the book "Charlotte's Web" I named the little heifer Charlotte. For the non-farm reader, a heifer is a girl calf.

I was very proud of my very own calf and showed little Charlotte off to every friend and relative that visited. My great-aunt Emma was one of the relatives that I dragged out to see Charlotte.

Years later I heard from family members that Aunt Emma had been less than excited about my naming my Jersey "Charlotte." By then, I was in high school and Charlotte was no longer a part of my herd. Aunt Emma's attitude may have been due to the fact that her mother was named Charlotte, or that was what I was told. Years later while doing some research on genealogy I found that Aunt Emma had one child, a daughter that she had named Charlotte. That little Charlotte only lived a little over two years.

In retrospect, I am glad that Aunt Emma never mentioned it to me and that I just thought that she wasn't excited by cows.

About six years later I had added a Shorthorn cow to my herd. That shorthorn had a little heifer calf that I named Juliana. I don't remember why I choose that name for the calf. I do remember that I bragged to most of my relatives, including Aunt Emma.

Once again years later, I heard that Aunt Emma hadn't been happy that I would name a calf after her sister. Juliana had been her older sister and had died long before Aunt Emma had been born, but knowing the family, I do understand now.

The years rolled by and I found myself married and the father of two boys. My wife was pregnant and I was hoping for a girl. We had agreed with the names with the first born, Benjamin for a boy and Charlotte for a girl. Now we had Ben and Jacob and were hoping that we'd need pink blankets so that we could use Charlotte.

As a young man, I wanted to honor the family and really liked the name Charlotte. Both of my grandmothers (Alta and Nellie) had given me strict instructions that no child of mine was to be saddled with their names and my wife didn't want to give a girl either of her grandmother's (Adelaide and Vida Mae) names. Since great-grandma had carried the name, and my wife liked it, that was settled.

When the big day arrived, I was excited to find the newest member of our family was a little baby girl that was given the name of Charlotte Mae.

Soon the snickers were heard at family gatherings. It became a family joke that I'd named my daughter after my cow. Years after Aunt Emma had passed on, the story grew that I'd named my cow after my great-grandmother and then named my daughter after the cow.

As a leader, you must develop a sense of humor. I am a farm boy at heart and naming a child after a cow isn't going to happen. But it makes a funny story and a great way to make people smile, if not laugh.

If you can't laugh at yourself, you will find that leadership has many unpleasant moments. Yet those moments will disappear forever when you can laugh with your fellow members.

I may not have named my daughter after a cow, but I'm sure that my grandchildren will hear the humorous story of how I did.

Inclusion

On the farm, we'd occasionally purchase a Holstein calf to help keep one of our cows from getting mastitis. Mastitis is a disease that affects the milk and milk production and is often caused by too much milk being produced by the cow and not enough being drank by the calf.

To remedy this, we'd buy a Holstein calf from a local dairy and put it as a second calf on the cows that were heavy milk producers. Once in a great while, we would end up with an extra calf and it would become a bottle baby. We had a small calf shed which was moved near the house so that we didn't have to walk far to feed the calf every morning and evening.

We also had chickens on the farm. They were large white chickens probably Leghorns, which produced eggs for the farm and when they stopped laying became dinner. However, once in a while, my mother would get an idea and we have something different for a while. We had a few Araucanas chickens because the eggs were blue. Once we even had a little Bantam or Banty hen.

This story is about the little Banty hen that we had and a Holstein bottle-baby calf.

The Banty hen was the only chicken not confined to the chicken house and the fenced in chicken yard. She wandered as she saw fit. It is likely that we tried to keep her with the other chickens, but she could fly a bit higher and further than the rest and as a result, the fence was not adequate to stop her.

As the weather was good, the calf was let out of the calf shed and allowed to roam the apple orchard during the day. This let him stretch his legs and explore the world that every young calf finds new and interesting.

One day we noticed the calf following the Banty hen around. We were curious about what would happen when the calf got too close to the hen. Then that little hen walked up to the calf and gave a little peck on its nose.

We realized that the little Banty hen had adopted the Holstein calf as part of its brood. Since she didn't have little fuzzy chicks, the hen had decided the big black and white calf was hers to mother. She had the calf following her around the orchard as if it was just another chick that she was raising.

The lesson was simply that you can include people by choice. They don't have to look just like you, they don't have to speak the same way, you just must choose to include them. Imagine how much easier it is for you to include someone in your group, than it was for a tiny little hen to include a large Holstein calf as part of her family.

Treating people as part of the group isn't always easy, but it is ultimately a choice that you and your fellow members have complete control over.

That little hen did find out that not everyone one viewed the world the way she did. The day came when the herd was let into the pasture next to the orchard. To introduce the calf to the herd, we turned him into the pasture with the cows for the day.

I'm sure he was excited to get to play with calves his own age, and he was probably a bit nervous around the full-grown cows. But when the gate was opened, he willingly entered the pasture.

That little Banty hen was not happy that her baby was mingling with the herd of cattle. She went into the field and was making a fuss when one of the cows came over to check out the chicken. A moment later the cow decided that chickens didn't belong in the pasture and ran that chicken through the fence.

That little hen got the message and spent the rest of the day sitting on a fencepost telling the world that a loving mother hen didn't deserve to be treated that way. At the end of the day, the calf was back in the calf shed having a bottle with his mother hen looking out for him.

Time quickly passed and soon the calf was living with the herd and the hen was looking for other babies to take care of.

The lesson of this portion of the story is that you don't have control over other people's actions. You may include others in your group, but that doesn't mean others will treat you the same way. Just as that cow didn't include the hen in the herd, others will sometimes not include you for reasons you may not understand. However, it doesn't stop you from talking to them and learning why you're not being included.

Inclusion is about how you choose to include others. If you judge others by their words, actions, and character you will find many to be a part of your group. If you find a group that doesn't want to include you, ask why.

Leadership is about finding ways to include people on your team. Often the people are very different, but they are unified in purpose. Your task will be much easier than a Banty hen trying to adopt a Holstein calf.

Learning

As a Junior in high school I bought a 1966 Chevy pickup. It was the first vehicle that I had purchased by myself. I had been driving a 1967 Chevy Nova four-door sedan that had been given to my brother and I by my great-aunt May. I was excited by the fact that it was my truck.

The Chevy was mid-night blue with white bumper and mirrors. It had a big 292 six-cylinder engine with a 4-speed transmission and I was so proud of it. While many of my fellow high school students were trying to get cars with big V-8's, most of us in the FFA program were buying pickups.

During my senior year, the student paper decided to add a feature. While everyone knew the feature was designed to contrast the "hottest" car on campus with something not so "cool" I was still proud to have my truck featured as the "Mud and Manure Machine". Some might not see the fun, utility, and pride in a pickup, but I sure did.

One day the brakes began failing on that truck. My dad told me to take it into the dealership. I made the appointment and took it in. They informed me that the rear brakes were shot and quoted a first-class complete brake job that shocked me with the cost. When I asked about options, they told me that there were none, they would only do the job to their specs. Then they told me that they would not even put the tires back on the truck as it wasn't safe to drive.

I called my dad and soon he had negotiated a compromise. They would do a brake job without all the bells and whistles and the total bill would be about half of what they had quoted me.

I realized that I didn't know enough to argue with anyone and quickly agreed. I also realized that my dad did quite a bit of business with the dealership because he wasn't a mechanic either.

A few months later, I lost a bearing in the front wheel hub. I decided that I would fix this myself. I talked to the local mechanic in the community and then took the front wheel off the truck. I got the front hub and drum off with some work and found that the hub was damaged, but the spindle was fine.

I found a good used hub in a junk yard and returned home to install it. I then learned how to separate the brake drum from the hub, how to install a new bearing in the replacement hub, and how to reassemble the parts onto the truck.

What would have taken an experienced mechanic an hour or so, took me all weekend. At the end of the weekend, I was proud that I had fixed my truck. I'll admit that I had skinned a knuckle or two, had grease everywhere, and had half the tools on the farm scattered around my truck.

I had learned how to do something new that weekend. The motivation was to be independent and to take care of my own problems, as well as to save some money. What I didn't realize at the time was that confronting problems will often give you great opportunities to learn something new.

Over time, I learned more about how cars worked. Eventually, I had the opportunity to work as a mechanic and became certified in several areas of mechanical expertise. While I chose to get out of the automotive repair field, the skills have remained valuable to me in keeping my cars and trucks running. Those skills have also enhanced my efforts to restore classic vehicles.

The greatest benefit was the realization that you will learn as you go. As a leader, you don't have to know how to deal with every problem before you face it. You can and will learn as you experience different problems.

Your education will include the sharing of problems and solutions with other leaders, the occasional book, article or seminar on leadership, and good old trial and error. Your experiences will combine these different lessons into your own personal leadership style.

A constant refrain that I hear is "Imagine what we could have done during my term if I had known at the beginning what I know now." When you do the job, you are going to learn a great deal about yourself and leadership. Your leadership skills will grow far more than you imagine due to learning on the job.

While you may never have to replace the front hub on a 1966 Chevy pickup, you will have the opportunity to learn how to be a better leader by dealing with the problems and challenges of leadership.

No

I can't count the number of times on the farm I've heard or said, "No" or more accurately, "Noooo". When the cows were headed towards a gate that was left open, when a dog went running after a cat, or someone was about to make a mistake. I know that two-letter word (which does stretch under duress) has been said to me innumerable times over the years.

One hot August day at State Fair, while showing my shorthorns in FFA, it was a show day. With the excitement, the heat, and the crowds, all of the animals were stressed. One young advisor saw a big sow (momma pig) that was starting to exhibit signs of being overheated. Pigs don't have sweat glands to keep them cool during hot days, which makes them susceptible to heat stroke.

I and about 50 others saw that young teacher grab a pail of water and as he dowsed down that pig as a chorus of "Noo's" came from around that area. That poor pig dropped dead from shock when that cold water drenched it. While the teacher tried CPR on that big sow, it was unsuccessful. I am sure that the owner of the pig, that young teacher, and so many more people were hurt, or angered by the unfortunate and well-intended act.

Leaders need to understand that the word "no" has several purposes. The first that I've illustrated is to protect. We say no to pets, to children, and to adults to protect them. Sometimes it is our job to say no, as in a crossing guard at a school, who tells both children and drivers when they can cross or go and when they must stop and wait.

As a leader, it is your job to protect the rules. Depending upon your position, you may have to tell you fellow members that they cannot do something. An even harder task is to stop them when they are doing something that is contrary to the rules.

I remember one young woman in the Grange. She said yes to every request for help she got. She volunteered for every committee, she held several offices at different levels of the organization, and she promised something for just about every event or activity.

However, she often failed to meet her obligations. It wasn't for lack of trying, but with a job, a family, and commitments to several organizations, she was just stretched too thin. She would miss a deadline or double book a meeting. It was embarrassing to her and frustrating to her fellow members.

Her failing was that she had never learned to say no. A leader should try to recognize their limitations in time and talent. If you learn to say no to people so that you can accomplish the tasks that are on your plate; you will have learned an important and powerful lesson. That doesn't mean others should set your limits, but that you should set them based upon your own assessment of your abilities and time constraints.

Years ago, I had the responsibility of appointing various committees and representatives for the State Grange. I found that this was one of the most demanding aspects of team building. One member had held a position for quite a few years. In looking at his performance, I saw a member who was knowledgeable, pleasant and an obvious choice. The only problem was that no one was listening to him because he had been in the position for quite a while.

I called him and gave him the courtesy of telling him myself that he was not going to be reappointed and that I felt it was time for a new face and voice in that position. He was disappointed as he enjoyed the position that he had held.

I hoped that he would help me out in other areas, but he chose not to, and I knew that I had either angered or hurt him. About three years later, at the State Convention, I saw him coming to greet me with a big smile.

He grabbed my hand and as he shook it, he said, "thank you." He explained, that spring he realized that his fellow members were listening to him. He had not realized that they were tuning him out until they started listening to him again.

That moment where he realized that not appointing him was done for his good was powerful for both of us. For him, he realized the importance of having his fellow members respect and having them listen to his advice and observations. For me, it was that when you do the right thing for the organization and for the members, it will usually work out.

Saying no, as a leader, is sometimes the way we help others to grow, to learn, and sometimes it is a way to give them that critical time to learn to be better leaders.

The other issue to be aware of is the tendency of leaders who are comfortable in saying no first and then thinking through the issue. My brother-in-law once suggested an idea in a meeting and an influential leader stood and gave his reasons why the idea should not be adopted. With that, the idea was rejected by the majority. After the meeting, that leader approached my brother-in-law and said that on reflection, maybe he had been wrong and the idea had merit.

The trouble with moments like this is that your group can lose a member if you just say no. It can also discourage members from continuing to grow as leaders. With great influence comes the responsibility to make sure that you do not have a knee-jerk reaction to ideas and suggestions.

People never like to be told no. Regardless of whether you are protecting, guiding, or drawing boundaries for your members, it is your task as the leader to say no on occasion. When you can give options to a member when you must say no to something, it can assist you greatly in your team building efforts.

Take the time to reflect on your own leadership skills and available time. Learn to say no to things that you are not passionate about, or do not have the time for. Take on the challenges that will stretch and grow you and give others the opportunity to learn and grow doing those things that you have already mastered.

No is not a bad word, it is an important word that needs to be used carefully.

Optimism

Growing sweet corn was one of the many tasks on the farm. Corn on the cob for the family and corn stalks for the cows were the reward for all the work.

The corn patch or field was an area down by the creek. The irrigation mainline pipe went through the field so water was easy to apply. Each fall we spread manure on the ground to ensure that the soil was ready to grow corn the next spring.

The process started each spring with my dad hooking up to the plow to the tractor and turning over the ground in the corn patch. After he plowed, he would disk and harrow the field so that we could lay out the rows of corn.

We used an old corn planter and we would walk along the row and plant the kernels of corn at regular intervals. Then we would wait for the corn to push its green shoots out of the soil.

Once the corn spouted, then the real work would begin. Each of us kids would regularly be given a hoe and would have to spend a morning or afternoon hoeing the corn. In layman's terms, we were the weed control. My parents were not opposed to chemicals with which to control weeds, it was just a lot cheaper to have kids weed the corn patch with hoes. They also told us that doing chores like hoeing, built character.

Weeding never ended. With the rich soil and the regular watering of the corn, it was ideal for weeds as well. Until the corn was harvested, weeding was a part of the farm routine for all of us kids.

As the corn grew, we would regularly have to set up the irrigation pipe to provide water to the growing plants. Moving the pipe became harder every day as the corn grew taller, you had to lift the pipe higher to prevent breaking the corn stalk. When the corn attained its full height, it took two of us, one lifting each end of the pipe to move the pipe in the corn patch.

As the corn matured, we had to watch the edges of the corn patch for sign that a nutria or muskrat had moved into the creek and had begun harvesting our corn. Nutria and muskrats are just big rodents who built dens along the edges of the creek and can consume a lot of corn in a short time.

When we saw that one of these rodents had moved into the area and was raiding our corn patch, we would either watch for a shot at them with the .22 rifle or set a trap for them. A varmint could raid our corn patch for a while, but sooner or later they would either get caught or move out looking for friendlier neighbors.

Once the corn was ripe; every day we would select ears for dinner and when Mom was ready to preserve a batch, we pick a lot of it. After we picked the ears, we cut the stalks and fed them to the steers which were being fed to prepare them for market.

Raising sweet corn took optimism. A lot of work was needed before you saw the first sign of growth. Then more work was needed to give the growing corn plant the best opportunity to produce full ears of corn. Even the harvest took work.

All this work was fueled by optimism. The hope of the tasty ears of corn to be enjoyed at the dinner table. The hope of supplementing the feed for the steers that were being fed for market.

Optimism is a critical component of leadership. If you don't have hope and a positive image of the future, you are not going to do the things necessary to create that future.

Optimism is as contagious as a negative attitude. If you infect your members with optimism, your teams will accomplish great things.

You may not have to hoe a corn patch, but as a leader, you will need to cultivate the soil of whatever organization you are leading with optimism.

Perseverance

In the Pacific Northwest, there are some huge trees and on the farm where I grew up, there were some huge stumps. Those stumps were 6 to 10 feet in diameter and still had the notches where springboards had been put to allow the loggers to stand 10 to 15 feet off the ground to cut above the base of the tree.

As a young teen, I volunteered to cut down a tree that my dad wanted removed. It was less than two feet through and I considered myself a budding logger. Instead of using the chainsaw, I decided to do it old school and use the doubled bitted axe. For those that don't know axes, single bit axes have one cutting edge and a double bit axe has two cutting edges.

Cutting down a tree with a standard axe isn't anything like you can see at a timber festival or on TV and I was about to find out why.

Gathering a good pair of leather gloves, a jug of water, and grabbing my trusty axe, I proceeded to the tree. It was on a hillside and stood fairly straight. I thought to myself, a notch on the downhill side and that tree will fall down the hill where my dad wanted it.

I swung that axe at the point where I wanted to notch the trunk and realized immediately that there were no big chips of wood flying as a result of my mighty blow. That big tree absorbed each blow and while I was cutting into the trunk, I realized that the chips were going to be a lot smaller than anticipated.

The notch slowly grew as I nibbled each chip from the tree trunk. I soon lost count of how many blows I delivered, but the notch continued to grow with each chip that I dislodged. What I thought should take but a minute or two turned into 10 or 15 minutes of steady work.

I tried using the other bit on the axe and soon decided that one side was slightly sharper than the other. Trouble was that they look the same and if I didn't pay attention, I would find myself using the duller side.

Finally, I decided that my notch was large enough and positioned correctly to ensure that the tree would fall in the desired location. I took a healthy drink of water, as the sweat was now pouring off me. I wondered if I should take a break and sharpen the axe, but decided that the hard part was over and I'd sharpen the axe later after the tree was down.

I stepped to the other side of the tree and began swinging that axe with as much power as I could. While I didn't hit where I aimed every time, soon there was a growing pile of little chips. I worked steadily with sweat dripping off me. After a while, I paused for a drink and surveyed the tree.

I realized that this job was going to take a bit longer than I had bargained for. Yet once started, the job had to be completed, if for nothing else than safety and pride. With a sigh, I picked up the axe and continued cutting chips out of that big tree trunk.

When I took my next water break, the tree trunk had a deep notch on the downhill side and a deep cut out of the uphill side. I knew the tree had to be getting close to losing its battle with gravity, but I no longer thought that this was an easy job.

Picking up the axe, I continued my assault on what I now viewed as a mighty tree. Suddenly the tree quivered. I stopped and stepped back. The tree gave a great creak and then nothing happened.

I waited a moment, but nothing else happened. I began swinging that axe again. Soon I was rewarded with more cracking sounds and the tree began to slowly lean down the hill. I stepped back as I was aware of the dangers that falling trees can pose. The tree slowly shifted and then accelerated toward the ground as gravity overwhelmed the strength of the small bit of wood that remained of the trunk.

The sound of that tree hitting the ground was better than the cheers of a crowd. It signified that I too, was man enough to be a logger. I will admit that I fired up the chainsaw to limb and cut that tree into firewood. I might have believed I was a tough logger, but I wasn't stupid.

The lesson that I learned was that perseverance is a necessary part of every task. You may have an idea of what needs to be done, how much work it will take, and how long it will take to complete the task; but at some point, you'll need to persevere in order to achieve success.

The easiest tasks can provide challenges that will frustrate you. The big jobs can threaten to overwhelm you, but perseverance is what will get you through that job. Call it sticking to it, never giving up, or even not being willing to admit defeat, persevere in every task and you will experience success as a leader.

Persistence

I remember one of the first independent jobs my parents gave me was digging postholes for a new fence. My great-aunt had passed away and my parents had inherited the 28 acres she owned. One of the things that needed to be done was put a fence in between that property and the adjoining property owned by my grandmother. The fence line ran among the cedar and fir trees down a long hill that ended in a stream.

The hardest part of building a fence is digging the holes. If you're digging in rich soil without rocks and roots the job goes quickly with a clamshell posthole digger. Once you have a hole, you set the post into the hole, fill the hole and tamp the dirt around the post and move to the next one. Once you've got the line of posts set, then you roll out the wire, tighten it and secure it to the post.

In the normal way of farm kid labor, my parents offered me the opportunity by setting the price at 10 cents a posthole. Being an eager young capitalist and knowing my parents would provide me with gloves and tools I accepted.

The first hole went quickly and I set a post in the hole and then paced out the distance to the next hole. However, it didn't take too many holes to run into the trees. Soon I was spending more time cutting my way through roots than in removing dirt from the holes.

The thought did cross my mind that I might find some type of treasure lost for decades in one of the holes. After a few more holes, my thoughts turned from treasure to just getting each hole to the right depth so that I could set that post.

I remember my parents making a comment or two about the straightness of my fence, but they didn't argue with the fact that some of the trees required a slight zig or zag. As my initial time table disappeared due to roots I wondered if 10 cents per hole was really worth it. Yet I knew that I had agreed to those terms so I counted each post set and how many were left to dig.

It was a relief to finish the fence line and have my parents help stretch the wire. There was a great deal of satisfaction in creating a strong fence.

I learned persistence doing that job. The realization that even easy jobs could become difficult and require persistence became a critical lesson to me as a leader.

Years later, I was offered my first real job so that I didn't have to pick strawberries. I had gotten my driver's license on my birthday in March and near the end of the school year, my former German teacher asked me if I wanted a job for the summer. As luck would have it, he wanted a fence built on a farm he had inherited out of Amity.

I was confident that with my experience I could build a straight and stout fence. What I didn't know about Amity was that the ridge he wanted to build the fence on was laced with rocks. I spent much of that summer digging postholes with those clamshell diggers, a shovel, and a big heavy screwdriver.

Every hole was started with the digger and then you'd hit a rock. The rocks were often too big to get out with the digger, so you'd pry them lose with the screwdriver. Lifting the rock out of the hole, you could then take a little more dirt out until you bumped into the next rock. Occasionally, you would find a really big rock and have to widen the hole to get the rock out. Once or twice, I just gave up and dug another hole a foot or two closer to the previous post.

Through persistence I built that fence and gained confidence that I could work the same as any man. As a leader, I look back at the experience gained by taking on a big job and finding it much harder than anticipated. The challenge and gallons of sweat expended made completion much sweeter.

During that summer I realized that my boss was a great teacher, but not really much of a farmer. I gained respect for him as he often pitched in to help me loosen rocks and get them out of the hole.

Because he was paying me, I thought I should be doing the bulk of the work, after all, it was my job.

However, as a leader, I look back and see that while I was persistent, maybe even a bit stubborn, he was concerned with his team, even though it was a team of one and he wanted to make the task easier.

Reflection has taught me that when a team is persistent they are unstoppable. The job may be difficult, the task may be filled with obstacles and trials, but the spirit of persistence will allow the individual and the team to find a solution, no matter how many postholes need to be dug.

Perspective

As a leader, you need to develop perspective. You should understand that what others see may be very different than what you see.

As a sophomore in high school, I learned a lesson on perspective.

Among my activities, I was a budding photographer. I started in grade schools with a simple 126 and over time upgraded to an SLR 35 mm camera. Over the years, I took stacks of photographs on the farm and even started developing and printing my own black and white photos.

Being a farm boy, whenever I had the chance to watch our local veterinarian work on our livestock I took the opportunity. Being a small operation, we didn't have the vet out much as we learned to pull calves, give shots, and do a lot of other preventative medicine ourselves.

However, one day a cow was having a particularly hard time giving birth. My parents were worried about losing the cow or calf and called the vet. Doctor Kimball was soon there.

He diagnosed the problem, and soon was pulling the calf. While he was working, I had grabbed my camera and was taking picture after picture.

For those who have never witnessed the miracle of birth, it is mixture of wonder and mess. There are a lot of liquids, mucus, and membranes, especially when you have a one hundred-pound calf.

That day the vet was able to help the cow out and soon a healthy calf was lying on the barn floor. The vet quickly wiped the calf's nose clean and made sure it was breathing.

If I remember correctly, that calf was trying to stand almost right after being born. In short order, it was standing even as it wobbled a bit. It was trying to find its first meal and its momma was trying to lick it clean.

Everyone had a big smile as every birth on the farm is worrisome until the calf is eating, and the cow is recovering. Then the emotional high is wonderful. However, this is just the set up for the lesson I learned.

Over the next few days, I developed the film I had shot and then set up my darkroom and started printing the photographs. I discovered that I had caught many of the shots that I wanted. From the vet working to save the calf, to its delivery, and then its first moments as it stood and ate.

The next time we went to Newberg, I stopped at the vet's office and gave him a set of the pictures. He seemed to like them a lot although in retrospect, I'm not sure whether he was being kind or if he truly liked them.

However, his praise was more than enough for me. I was a proud photographer and decided to share them with my fellow FFA members.

That term the first class I had with some of my friends was English. The English teacher was a great teacher and she was an older lady, likely in her 40's. (It is amazing how your perspective of older changes so rapidly, but that is another story.)

As class proceeded, we had some time to do some reading. I used the lull in class to pass the pack of photos to my classmate. The teacher caught us as he passed back the photos and came striding to the back of the classroom where we were sitting. She held out her hand and said, "let me see those."

Being a proud photographer, I handed them to her with a smile. She took one look at them and turned white as a ghost. When she handed them back, she quietly and firmly told me to never bring those pictures into her class again.

In reflecting about this incident, it is probable that she anticipated photos that teenage boys would have did not included the birthing of a calf. Experience has also since taught me that not everyone reacts to the miracle of birth, or other messy things, the same way.

The lesson learned was that you need to be aware of the different perspectives that people have of the same incident. Some people will only see the mess and miss the miracle. Others will miss all the detail and only see the miracle. A few will turn their eyes away and not see anything.

Remember that perspective is unique to each of us and your task as a leader is the communicate well enough to share your perspective with others. You also must try to see their perspective so that you understand what their objections or ideas are.

Learn to see what someone else sees and it will widen your perspective. That wider perspective will serve you well as a leader.

Pride (in Yourself)

Charlotte was my 4-H Jersey project. She was a black Jersey instead of one of the tan varieties. A black Jersey is a dark brown and has a reddish stripe down the backbone. Charlotte had a small udder, yet I know that she produced as much milk as any other Jersey.

Charlotte looked like any other cow on the farm. A bit of dirt caked here or there, a coating of dust on her hair, and some dirt or manure around at least one foot.

Charlotte and I practiced for the fair for many hours each year and while there were moments that she would disagree about what we were doing; she always came around to my instruction and guidance.

For the non-farmers, when you show cattle, the feet go in specific places to highlight certain aspects of the animal. With dairy cattle, heifers (the girls) and the cows (momma's) the legs are positioned differently.

One of the other things that show stock learn to accept is to have baths, get trims to highlight certain traits, and generally to be as polished as their owner can get them. Charlotte liked baths, mostly. I think it was the rubdown that she really enjoyed. She put up with the clippers and scrubbing as we trimmed her into a Jersey beauty with shining hooves.

What we learned about Charlotte was that she was a good-looking cow until she got to County Fair. Then when people were looking at her, she straightened out her back as if she knew everyone was looking at her, and she looked great. It was if she had seen the comic strip where the cow went from sway-back old cow to beautiful model cow.

It was commented to me several times how much better she looked in the show ring than back home in the pasture. It didn't matter how she knew it was show time, but she never went into the ring for judging looking any less than her best.

Due to her small udder, she never placed anywhere but near the bottom of the class in confirmation. While I understood the judge had no idea how much milk she actually gave, I sometimes wonder if Charlotte was as forgiving towards the various judges. But when you're a Jersey, the real judging is on the appearance of milk production not how sharp you look everywhere else.

The lesson for every leader is to simply to put your best foot forward. Take the time to comb your hair, shave, or put on make-up before you go into the world. Unlike a Jersey cow, your show ring is much bigger and more frequent than the one at County Fair.

Think about who is going to be looking at you. Dress to impress; clean, neat, and tidy never go wrong. You can be yourself and let people know that you take pride in yourself. You need to believe that you are worth it and then as a leader, you'll bring honor and pride to your fellow members and organization.

Charlotte liked being the center of attention and when it mattered, was the best Jersey cow she could be. Remember that you are on exhibition far more often as a leader than Charlotte ever was at County Fair.

Principles

To me, principles are those core elements of how you live your life, how you treat others, and what you believe in. They are the part of you that guides how you live and interact with the rest of the world. You may slip up once in a while, but you should never abandon or compromise your principles.

Your ethics, your values, your moral compass or belief of right and wrong come from the principles that you choose to adopt. Mine came from the teachings and example of my parents, my grandparents, and my faith.

Doing what is right has been ingrained in me since my childhood. As an adult through experience and observation, I have learned that principles can have moments where they are difficult to keep.

I once attended a conference where appointed representatives of the leader of the organization and other elected officers were provided training and guidance in their duties. The conference stressed the importance of following the rules and the importance of the procedures of the organization. I had the good fortune to attend because my wife was an officer.

The night before the conference was to start, the local unit had a meeting. The hall was filled with leaders from around the state. The meeting started well and it members were enjoying the fellowship.

However, then the local President announced that they had two new members and even though it was against the rules, they were going to induct them without the required process. They proceeded to induct the two into membership and while there was a lot of muttering around the hall, no one stood and said a single word.

The State President was noted for his adherence to the process of initiation for new members, yet he said nothing that night other than he wished that they had not done it. The next day, at the conference, he acted as if nothing had happened.

Over the two days of the conference, I heard several members comment on the fact that a local President had flaunted the rules in front of everybody, including the State President and that nothing had happened.

After that incident, the State President remained a well-like leader, but there were many who questioned his commitment to his professed principles towards the prescribed processes of the organization.

As a leader, you must be true to your core principles. In addition, you must be true to the core principle of the organization that you lead. Due to that one meeting, the leadership learned that conflict was too high of a price for adherence to the principles of the organization as written in the rules, at least in the eyes of their leader.

If principles are not worth potential conflict, the expenditure of money, or some other cost; what are principles worth? If doing the right thing is situational, then most would believe that it is not a principle. While conflict or strife should never be the goal of leaders, if you surrender your principles to avoid such problems you will be telling others that those "so-called" principles really are just empty words. The realities of principles are that you either live them or they don't exist.

As a leader, your adherence to your principles will set the example for your membership. Your actions in relation to the principles of the organization will make them relevant and current. This is one rule of leadership that has great power.

Principled leadership has its price, but it is a price that every leader should be willing to pay.

Responsibility

On the farm, there are many duties that become a responsibility for someone in the family. One of those responsibilities was changing the irrigation pipe.

Every morning and every evening, we had to move the irrigation line. The farm had a mainline of 4-inch pipe running along the center fence from the creek to the end of our property. Using valves, we almost always had two lines going, one on each side of the mainline.

Each sprinkler line consisted of pipe that was 2 inches in diameter and the longest were 40 feet long. Between each pipe was a sprinkler.

To change the pipe, you would turn off the water with the valve on the mainline and move the valve to the next mainline connector. Then you would flip up the latch on the far side of the sprinkler and unhook the pipe and move it into position with the valve.

When I was a little kid, two of us would work together, one at each end of a pipe. When we had grown enough to do it by ourselves, we'd lift the pipe from near the middle, allowing for the sprinkler weight, and pull it out of the pipeline and take it to the repositioned line. You would aim the end of the pipe into the sprinkler and push it into the sprinkler until it latched.

Once you were big enough to move pipe by yourself, you learned that you couldn't dig the end of the pipe into the ground. If you did, the sprinklers would likely plug up from the grass or dirt and you would have to clear them out when the water was running. On a hot day, it sounded refreshing, but we learned that sometimes you still had to turn the water off and remove the nozzle from the sprinkler to clear it of grass or mud.

You also learned to be careful as pipe can flex a great deal, but once it bends the crease is permanent. Over the years, damaged pipe was cut and made into shorter sections, but our parents worked hard to ensure that we understood, bent pipe was not acceptable.

Normally, a day or two after the cattle had grazed that pasture, one of the sprinkler lines was ready to enter that pasture. The grass got a good watering right after it had fed the cows. Then a week or so later, the second line would be in position to water that pasture again. By the time the cows were let into that pasture again, the grass would be lush and thick.

Most of the pastures had two settings of irrigation to provide adequate coverage. Between each pasture was an electric fence. When we were little, the fences were always turned off when it was time to change pipe. When we began to change pipe by ourselves, we always turned off the fence.

However, as I grew taller, I realized that I could just step over the fence without touching it. One day I decided to save a little time by not turning the electric fence off. Fear and challenge allowed me to change the irrigation that day with no repercussions.

Soon it was a regular point that I didn't turn the fence off except for a few fences that were a bit higher than average. Then the day came where I brushed the fence wire with the wet aluminum pipe. I learned that an electric fence bit a lot harder when you were holding wet aluminum pipe than it seemed to when you just accidently touched it.

One day I was showing off to my mother how I could step over the fence and pointing out the fact that her height prevented her from doing so. Suddenly I stumbled and dropped that pipe on the fence. I look at my mom, and realized that the wet aluminum pipe was lying on the fence. She just looked at me and said that it was my responsibility to get that pipe off the fence.

I took a deep breath and tried to quickly lift one end of the pipe up, hopefully to clear the fence. I felt the jolt of electricity, but in a moment the pipe was off, and I continued with the task of moving the pipe.

I learned responsibility from changing irrigation pipe. The cows needed grass to feed themselves and to produce enough milk for the calves to grow healthy and strong. It was our responsibility to ensure that the grass was healthy and nutritious for the cows. We could see the benefit of water on the grass and it was because we took responsibility to see that the grass was watered, that our cows were healthy.

We also learned responsibility in how we took care of the expensive part of the irrigation process. Pipe and sprinklers were costly and we learned how to prevent damage and protect the different components.

One of the important lessons of responsibility was the use of water. We followed science and common sense. We limited the amount of water with the number of hours at each setting and we did our best to use only as much water as required to keep the pastures green and lush.

Every leader needs to learn responsibility. Not just in performing their task, but in being part of the team. Correct problems, help out others, and realize that every job has importance. You may not have the opportunity to help by grabbing a section of pipe and help get it over a high fence, but you will have the chance to help others in some manner.

Leaders need to have the responsibility to see that the right things are done, the right way, and for the right reasons. Accept the responsibility and become a better leader. Just as the cows depended on our family changing the irrigation pipe, your organization is depending on you to lead.

Team

I spent much of each summer in the hay fields. At age eight, I could depress and hold both the brake and clutch on an old 1949 McCormick-Deering tractor. That summer I became a part of the haying crew by driving the tractor while my parents and others loaded the bales onto the trailer.

The next summer, my little brother proved his ability to do my job and I found myself promoted to bucking bales. Being a tall skinny kid, I quickly learned that handling hay bales isn't so much about brute strength, but leverage and momentum. Using your legs, you get the bale moving and then it is about keeping it moving as you guide it onto the stack.

As I got older, my parents gave me the opportunity to run the rake which windrowed the hay or turned over the wet hay in the windrow. Then I had the opportunity to learn to run the haybine (the machine that cuts and crimps the hay so that it dries quicker). Learning how to operate the baler finished out my education in the hay field.

No matter which machine you used, at the end of the process you ended up with a field of hay bales in long rows. To move the hay from field to barn, normally we drove the tractor and trailer through the field in low gear and at least one of the crew walked on each side of the trailer. They would pick up bales and toss them onto the trailer in a neat stack. Much of the time one of the neighbors would help and then someone stood on the trailer and stacked the load seven or eight bales high.

Once the trailer was loaded, the task switched from loading the hay onto the trailer to unloading the hay into the barn. The bottom of the stack was easy, each worker grabbed bales and started building a layer. As the stack grew, each layer was placed so that it tied the bales together into a solid stack and soon we would need the elevator to lift the bales from the trailer to the top of the stack. The hay elevator is just a long conveyer that lets an electric motor do the lifting. Usually one elevator keeps two stackers very busy.

While the job was always dusty and hard, you could see the result in fewer bales in the field and in the growing stack of hay bales in the barn. When it was hot, you drank a lot of water and had some potato chips to replenish the salt in your system.

However, when it clouded up and appeared ready to rain, the pace intensified. It is not desirable to get baled hay wet. In fact, it is quite dangerous. Wet hay heats up as it rots and there have been many barns that have burnt to the ground just because of wet hay being stacked in them.

Thankfully, on those occasions when we were racing the clouds to get the last few loads of hay in, it was usually a bit cooler. This was the moment where everyone on the crew knew that their effort counted. The team worked a bit faster, we stacked each load a little higher, and if necessary, we worked a little further into the night.

We were committed to getting the hay into the barn dry because we understood that it was both at its peak nutritional content and would last until needed during the winter, provided it stayed dry. The lesson that I learned was that everyone on the team worked hard to get the hay into the barn. Everyone on the hay crew team had a part to fulfill in that effort. Even when that effort became a race to beat damp weather, no one was unimportant.

The lesson that I learned was that the hard tasks in life are best accomplished with the help of a team. The person driving the tractor, the person standing on a slick trailer stacking the load, the people tossing bales on the trailer are all important. On the other end of the task, the person putting bales on the elevator and the workers stacking the hay are indispensable to the process.

No matter how tired we were when that last load went into the barn, a wave of relief and satisfaction would sweep through me. We'd beaten the rain and got the hay in dry. On those occasions where we ran out of time before the rain started, we kept working until the bales started sucking in the moisture. Then we waited for the rain to stop and the sun to return. No matter how wet a hay season was, we were committed to getting the hay in for the winter. It required a commitment from everyone on the team that lasted all summer.

We might have had to work on Sunday after church, or on a holiday, but that growing stack of hay in the barn was proof that it took a team for our farm to be successful.

Leadership is about building teams. Teams will accomplish far more than the most talented individuals. When the clouds boil up in the distance and you see obstacles in your way, your commitment to building teams will pay off as your team helps you get through the tough times.

You will find that building teams often takes more time initially, but in the end the results justify the effort. The leaders that accomplish the most are always the leaders who build teams.

You may not have to race the clouds while bucking hay bales, but you will find that a team will get the job done.

Teamwork

On the farm, we had a small apple orchard. My grandma who lived across the road also had a small apple orchard. We even had an apple tree in the middle of an alfalfa field. Many of our neighbors had small orchards and most had a least one tree. Apples were all around us in Scholls.

Each Autumn we would make apple cider. My parents had a cider press that they had bought used. It ground up the apples and then you'd use a screw press to squeeze all the juice out of the pulp.

When I was about eleven, my parents joined the local Grange. The Grange had a country store fund-raiser each fall where they sold rummage and ran the kitchen where they sold hamburgers, pies and more. Soon my parents and their fellow Grangers had added apple cider for sale at the country store.

Within a few years, making cider had become quite an operation. Some of the members saved glass gallon jugs. They would wash and sterilize the glass bottles that they accumulated. After the bottles were cleaned and ready, they would be put in boxes ready for filling.

Most of the members who had apple trees, would donate apples to the Grange. Those who didn't have apples trees, often had friends and neighbors who did and would solicit donations on behalf of the Grange. The members would take gunny sacks and fill them with apples in preparation for cider making.

A few days before the country store, we'd begin the process of making fresh apple cider. We set up the cider press under the deck so that we could work in a dry space (the deck made a covered area big enough to park cars or tractors in). We would clean and prepare the stainless-steel strainer, funnel, crock pots, and other necessary gear.

On the evening when we started, we would park a big wheel barrow near the press and mix hot and cold water together in it. We'd set a couple of wire buckets in the water and then the first bag of apples would be dumped into the water and were gently washed. The first team of members would begin with each of them taking an apple. Each apple was inspected and if it was a large apple, cut in half. Smaller apples were just tossed into the wire buckets. If there was a worm hole, the apple was cut open and the worm and its hole removed. They also removed any rotten spots. The good portion of the apple was tossed into the wire bucket and the wormy or bad portion was tossed into a five-gallon bucket set on the ground next to the wheel barrow.

When one of the wire buckets was nearly full, the electric motor on the cider press was plugged in and the process went into high gear. The apples were fed into the top of the grinder and apple pulp came out the bottom and filled wood press buckets. When the bucket was filled with apple pulp, one of the members would slide the bucket to the press and set the second bucket under the grinder where it would begin to fill.

The filled bucket was then matched up with the screw press and the squeezing out of the cider began. At the end of the tray, which held the press buckets, was a hole that allowed the cider to run into a pot that was inside a large pan. One person was responsible for pressing the apple pulp by turning the wheel on top of the screw. Another member would swap the pot when nearly full with an empty pot and take the pot of cider to the strainer. The cider was poured into the stainless-steel strainer and stored in a large crock pot.

One member spent their time changing the cheesecloth that was used to strain bits of apple out of the cider in the strainer and making sure that the crock pot didn't overflow. When it was filled, the strainer was moved to an empty pot.

When the pulp was squeezed as dry as possible, the pressure was released and the press retracted from the press bucket, the bucket was then lifted out and the apple pulp was put into another wheelbarrow.

The press bucket then took its place under the grinder and the process began again. The entire evening would be spent turning sacks of waiting apples into cider and apple pulp.

Waiting until the next day gave the fresh cider time to settle out anything the strainer had missed. Then a couple of members would take the fresh cider and pour it into the waiting glass jugs. We would take the apple pulp and put some around the rhododendrons for fertilizer and feed the rest to the cows.

With a team working together, many gallons of fresh apple cider could be made each evening and by the end of the week, hundreds of gallons of cider would be ready for sale.

Even though one person could have made cider, having a team working together allowed far more to be made in a short time. Each person had a task and even if people switched tasks, the process was expedited by many hands working together. Set up was always quicker with a dedicated crew; and clean up went much faster with the extra hands.

Teamwork was essential to making cider in substantial amounts. It didn't matter if you gathered apples, washed and cut them, fed the grinder on the press, or took the wheelbarrow of pulp to the cows. Each task was equally important in the process of turning apples into cider which benefited the projects that the Grange sponsored.

There were leaders who orchestrated this project, but each team member would pitch in where ever they were needed. After a night of cider making, the next night they might start doing a different task and no one argued. It was a group of Grange members (a team working together) who were focused on getting the job done; creating gallons and gallons of fresh cider to sell.

The lesson for each leader is that you need teamwork to accomplish all the tasks required. A style of teamwork where the members can assist each other and are willing to keep the focus on the goal rather than recognition. It is your job to learn to accept comments and ideas from your team and find ways to incorporate them into the team's actions.

Just as making cider is far easier with teamwork, being a leader is far easier when you have teamwork as the basis for your efforts. Teamwork is the crucial element of success.

Work Ethic

"You owe me a bucket of walnuts," were not the words I was expecting. I was a grade-school kid and was with my mom helping pick walnuts for Mr. Saxton. When I heard those simple words, I realized that I'd been caught playing, instead of working.

Under that big walnut tree, the walnuts had been arranged like a little army instead of piling up in the 5-gallon bucket when I was caught. My imagination had been working overtime and those walnuts made great toys.

I understood that harvesting the walnut crop was important and that we were paid for each bucket we filled. While I knew that the adults would expect me to pick up walnuts, what I hadn't counted on was that I could be fined for not working.

The obligation to work was an important lesson to a little boy. I finished that day by working steadily at filling that 5-gallon bucket many more times. In real terms that day, the game changed from using the walnuts as toys to one of clearing the ground of the walnuts. My imagination continued to work, but aligned with the task of filling buckets.

Mr. Saxton became a role model for me, one of many local farmers who showed me the value of a strong work ethic.

One of the reinforcing lessons on the importance of a work ethic that I learned was due to the corn patch and garden. It was one of the jobs of the kids on the farm to weed the garden and corn patch. I'm not sure why I didn't like weeding, but it was one of the few tasks that I really didn't like.

When you weeded with a hoe, you had to watch what you were doing so that you didn't harm the plant that you wanted to produce. You stirred the soil with the hoe, loosening the weed so that its roots were exposed to the sun. Then you knew that it would dry out and die, leaving the vegetables to grow and prosper.

Sometimes you had to get down on your hands and knees and pull each weed out. You'd grab it at the base of its stalk and pull. When the soil was damp or loose, they came right out. When the soil was drier or compacted, it depended upon what type of weed you were pulling. Some came out easily while others, having substantial tap roots, were a bit stubborn and required a deal of effort.

The fact that to weed without a hoe meant that I was either bent over pulling weeds or crawling on my hands and knees was a frustration. Herding cows, fixing fence, bucking bales and most other tasks on the farm were done standing. For whatever reason, I detested tasks like weeding which didn't involve much movement.

When you were weeding and the corn was waist high or higher, the corn leaves rubbed against you constantly. While it didn't hurt, for me it was a constant irritant, probably because I didn't want to be there anyway. The combination of lack of movement, being bent over, and other minor irritations made weeding the garden one of my least desirable activities.

Yet the job needed to be done and even as I got older, it remained one of the tasks that everyone had to participate in. It taught me that if you must do something that you don't like, just do it and get it over with. As I matured, I took pride in doing a quality job, even when I didn't want to do that task.

I learned that the walnuts needed to be harvested and delay could reduce their value. I learned that playing when time is short is not an option. When a task needs to be done, get it done and later there will be time to play.

The corn and other garden plants would have produced without weeding. However, they would not have produced nearly as much if we had allowed the weeds to compete for the available nutrients in the soil. A good work ethic means that you understand that even unpleasant tasks are often necessary to move you toward your ultimate goal.

Leaders must develop a strong work ethic because they should set the example for their team. They need to understand and communicate that the team's tasks are necessary to achieving the goal.

You may not have to pick up walnuts or hoe the garden, but as a leader, you have an obligation to your organization to put in the effort required to achieve growth and the goals of the group.

The Journey Continues

I hope you've enjoyed these stories from my youth and now take the time to reflect upon the importance of each lesson. If you've skipped to the end, you missed the best part.

The memories and experiences that I've shared mean a great deal to me. Thinking about Charlotte, George, and Trumpet brought a lot of emotions flooding home for me while writing their stories. For you, I hope they brought a smile and the realization that life is full of lessons we can learn from as we grow as leaders.

I am sure that each of you will discover lessons within your own life and I encourage you to share those lessons in your unique way. The best way to reinforce an important lesson is to share it with someone else.

Leadership is a learned skill and ever book and experience will aid you in your effort to improve that skill. I wish you well as your journey of leadership development continues.

To learn more about leadership development training by Ed Luttrell, visit: www.CornerPostLeadership.com

Other books by Ed to read:

Lessons from Rural America: Thoughts on Leadership, Integrity and Policy available at https://www.amazon.com/dp/B01AF0L1UC

Made in the USA
Columbia, SC
25 July 2018